A Hand
Full of Cards

By Jane Thomas

A Hand Full of Cards
9780956894731

Published by *Nosper Books* 2020
www.nosper.com

Copyright © Jane Thomas 2020

# Foreword

The story of my childhood is foremost a personal project. It may provide insights into my character and formative experiences, which have made my work on sexuality possible. It may also help the reader understand what has motivated me to work so hard and for so little reward in such a taboo area of the human experience.

In common with most people living in developed countries today, I grew up with all the essentials. The basics of survival (food, shelter and safety) were never a concern. I had good health and all my faculties. I was not abused physically or emotionally. Yet I felt deprived. Reconciling how we feel about our childhood is part of accepting our adult selves. We often assume that others had an easier start in life. But we rarely look at the whole picture. I have concluded that we all have different challenges. We are dealt a hand at the beginning and then it's about how we play out our cards.

I always knew my family was unconventional. No one ever explained why I could not live with my parents. I resented living with adults who were employed to look after me. So, although I was privately educated from a young age, I never considered myself to be privileged. My parents gave me little in terms of material possessions and domestic stability but they made me feel loved. For all their faults, as respectable citizens and their failings as responsible parents, Jo and Trevor had personal warmth. Uninhibited in exploring life's opportunities, they lived life without ever apparently worrying about what other people thought of them.

Consequently, I grew up looking for the positives in people. I don't believe in making excuses but I accept that life has its grey areas. It is not always squeaky clean. I was influenced by my love for my parents as well as by the social issues raised by the way in which they lived their lives. Other adults often treated us, as if we children were accountable for the misdeeds of our parents: their lifestyles and their choices that society disapproved of. Later I concluded that my parents struggled to cope with all the challenges that life threw at them. I was very fond of them and, loving my parents, helped me realise that morality should be less about judging others and more about accepting people for who they are. We are all so different. Love is more about what we give, than what we receive.

Talents and abilities are important but the over-riding factor in success must be our personal drive or motivation. Success in book-learning makes a person an academic. True intelligence encompasses our ability to make the most of our personal talents, to achieve personal contentment and to add value to the lives of those around us. Over the years, I have drawn great comfort from one of my father's sayings "Don't let the buggers get you down!" Whenever I feel demoralised, I remember that saying. It is so easy to criticise and so few people think to offer any praise. If you want to succeed, then don't listen to anyone telling you it's not possible.

I respect other people's religious beliefs and envy anyone who is comforted by the belief in a God of any religion. Perhaps because I had to be self-reliant during my childhood, I cannot believe in a super-being who oversees our earthly exploits. However, I do believe in the power of the human spirit and in that sense, I believe that God is the power within each of us to fight for good over evil. I don't see faith as an excuse for complacent self-righteousness. So often our greatest weaknesses are silence, apathy and inaction.

I like vegetarian food. I prefer to avoid killing animals but also a vegetarian diet helps me keep in shape. I accept that I am fortunate to live in an affluent society where we can worry about moral issues. But I am often shocked by people's lack of compassion and their disregard for the world we live in. If we are to preserve our world for future generations, rather than wasting our natural resources, we need to think more carefully about how we take care of our planet.

I have been married for over 30 years and I have three daughters. My hobbies include travel, languages, walking, cinema, history and cosmology. I have an Upper Second Honours degree (Maths) from Southampton University and I qualified as a Chartered Accountant (FCA). I worked as a finance manager in hi-tech companies for over 25 years. Recently I have also taught English as a foreign language.

Jane Thomas

Spring 2020

# Contents

| | |
|---|---|
| **PART I: MY EARLY YEARS** | 1 |
| Looked after by a nanny in Trevor's house | 1 |
| Holidays with Trevor and day outings with Jo | 5 |
| Visiting my father's parents in Durham City | 9 |
| A privileged education in the North of England | 13 |
| Boarding school indoor fun and outdoor games | 18 |
| Coping with discipline and standing up to authority | 23 |
| **PART II: MY MOTHER'S FAMILY** | 28 |
| The poverty and deprivations of the King family | 28 |
| The King children miss school to work in the fields | 32 |
| Jo leaves the Nissen hut and later marries Trevor | 36 |
| Trevor often absented himself from the marriage | 40 |
| The Hares use their money to end the custody battle | 44 |
| Holidays with Jo in the only home we ever knew | 49 |
| **PART III: MY FATHER'S FAMILY** | 54 |
| My paternal grandfather's family: The Hares | 54 |
| My paternal grandmother's family: The Waltons | 58 |
| Trevor's Cousin George and a trip to the Far East | 60 |
| Trevor's youth and failing his medical studies | 64 |
| My aunt Barbara and the Turnbull family | 67 |
| Holidays with Trevor and his family in the North | 71 |
| **PART IV: MY ADOLESCENCE** | 77 |
| The transition from prep school to senior school | 77 |
| The onset of puberty and surviving teenage crushes | 81 |
| Learning about relationships by living together | 86 |

| | |
|---|---|
| A chance to think about morality and spirituality | 90 |
| Academic competition and external examinations | 95 |
| School social dances and an introduction to men | 99 |
| **PART V: MY PARENTS** | **104** |
| Holidays with Jo and living the poor life | 104 |
| Jo's pride and resentment over our education | 109 |
| Learning about my father and my parent's divorce | 114 |
| Holidays with Trevor and living the rich life | 118 |
| A man's idea of a teenage sex education | 121 |
| Trevor, the silver spoon and his parents' money | 125 |
| **PART VI: OUT IN THE WORLD** | **129** |
| Sixth form college and meeting boys at last | 129 |
| Concerns about being accepted and an infatuation | 133 |
| Au-pairing in a chateau and vineyard in France | 138 |
| Taking time out to learn about working life | 143 |
| Au-pairing in Germany and rethinking religion | 149 |
| The kindness of strangers and thoughts on morality | 152 |
| **PART VII: POSTSCRIPT** | **156** |
| Finding my own way and meeting my life-partner | 156 |
| My father's illness and his ever-reducing capital | 160 |
| My mother's business and her drinking habit | 166 |
| The split with Sarah and reconciling personalities | 170 |
| Jo's children and the irony of illegitimacy | 174 |
| My quest to apply scientific principles to sexuality | 178 |

*To Jo and Trevor*
*for being the most interesting people*
*I have ever met and*
*for making me feel special as a child.*

'A Hand Full of Cards' tells the story of my childhood. It is a story I have wanted to write ever since I was a young child.

In the light of my work on sexuality, I have decided to be explicit about my emotional and sexual development as I was growing up. I think it is valuable to highlight how differently girls develop compared with boys.

Writing an autobiography involves considerable trepidation. I am very grateful to my family and friends who have responded so positively by contributing their own stories, which I have added to complement mine.

# PART I: MY EARLY YEARS

## Looked after by a nanny in Trevor's house

I was five years old when I went to live in my father's house in Battersea. My childhood companion, my sister Sarah, was three. We arrived as we were, with no belongings of any kind. Trevor's sister Barbara sent down a parcel of second-hand clothes that had belonged to her daughter Sue. Two years earlier, my parents had been living in Bayswater when my mother left. She took us with her and stayed with friends. But later Jo could find nowhere to live. So she told Trevor that he would have to have us. This action explained in part why legal custody was later awarded to Trevor.

Trevor had never found a job to suit him. He had been educated at boarding school and later at medical school with his parents pushing all the way. But he was not interested in a medical career. Finally, he dropped out and moved to London where he tried his hand at a variety of jobs. Trevor spent money easily but he had little motivation to earn any. He never succeeded in covering the costs of his extravagant lifestyle. His parents were rich so he was used to money always being there. Later he inherited various sums from rich relatives and this enabled him finally to own a property in his own name. He had the idea of earning money by renting rooms.

Trevor had let the lower ground floor of the house in Battersea to a middle-aged Scot, Noel, who became a life-long friend. No doubt he would have let the top floor flat as well but now he arranged for us to live there with a nanny. A series of women came and went in the early months. I remember a large Spanish woman who made an impression on me because she spoke so little English. Finally, he engaged an Irish woman called Daphne. She was a single parent in her mid-twenties with two boys of her own. Daphne looked after the four of us single-handed. She never smacked us but we lived in anticipation of her temper. I don't remember her showing any affection even towards her own children, Patrick and Christopher.

The flat had its own entrance from the top landing. Just inside was the door to the toilet. It was a cold, barren room with a chequered floor of black and white lino tiles. The white ceramic toilet with its high black cistern and long pull chain was at the far end. I remember Sarah being sent there sometimes, perhaps as a form of punishment. Further down the corridor was a narrow galley kitchen with a small built-in folding table against the wall. Sarah and I slept in twin beds in the bedroom on the far side of the kitchen. Patrick and Christopher slept in bunk beds in the smaller bedroom next to the lounge. While Daphne had to sleep on a sofa bed in the lounge.

The furniture was mostly second-hand from my father's family. The heavy floral curtains were cast-offs from my grandparents' home in Durham. There was no bath in the flat. The tiny shower cubicle with a corner basin was Daphne's room and we were not allowed in there. I have no memory of ever washing. When we got head lice, we took turns sitting in the kitchen sink while Daphne doused us down. One day after watching some programme on television, I asked Trevor why we never brushed our teeth. Later Daphne gave me a hard time for getting her into trouble. My father never appeared to consider the effect of his direct approach. He seemed oblivious to the fact that people inevitably retaliated by blaming me.

Patrick and Christopher were close to us in age. Patrick and I got along fine but Sarah always seemed to be at odds with Christopher. Trevor openly disapproved of the boys' behaviour. He liked to say: *"children should be seen and not heard"*. He was pleased that Sarah and I conformed to this Victorian picture of idyllic children. He liked to accept the inherent credit for nicely behaved children. Of course, girls were likely to be less boisterous than boys but we were too intimidated by our circumstances to be cheeky or badly behaved. There was a one girl at the local school who Daphne often singled out, claiming that she was dirty and always had head lice. For some reason, she would use this girl as a kind of threat, saying that if we did not mend our ways we would become like this girl.

There was a black and white television in the flat but in the 1960s there were few programmes for children. Adults certainly didn't feel obliged to play with children as they do today. We had few toys. I remember the boredom and how the days seemed endless. We had to invent our own amusements. Sarah and I spent hours copying cartoon characters from picture books. Once we were given some wool and we used pencils as knitting needles. Daphne's boyfriend Mike visited on weekends and I used to play poker with the adults. On fine summer days, Daphne took us all to Battersea Park and we picnicked on the grass or played in the playground.

Living apart from my parents made me needy for love and attention. But regardless of the circumstances, I was a demanding child. From a young age, I used to sulk for hours, driven by a stubborn determination to get my own way. Jo told me that I once locked myself in an upstairs bathroom and threatened to jump out of the window to win some childish battle of wills. I wanted to control my own fate. I also assumed I was as capable as anyone else of understanding any topic. I grew up trying to make sense of the adult world. I exasperated my parents by asking 'Why?' in reply to any explanation I did not understand. Often there were no answers.

Once I started school, I used to tell Sarah about everything I had learned from the day as we lay awake at night before going to sleep. On the mantelpiece there was a presentation bookcase of Beatrix Potter books. But I don't remember anyone reading to us. There was also a map of the world on the wall behind two lamps made from Mateus wine bottles. The paper behind the lamps was brown and I was always afraid that the paper would catch on fire. I used to ask for the lights to be switched off as soon as possible. Trevor dismissed my concerns as being trivial. Adults often fail to understand that small children have fears that are very real to them.

When she was six, Sarah also went to school. We were both quiet but artistic, which made us favourites of the teacher, Mrs Matthews. When we left the school, she took us out for the day to the park and gave us each a little rabbit soft toy. Mine was white and I called her Cottontail, after one of the sisters of Peter Rabbit from Beatrix Potter. Together with a larger teddy Trevor had given me, these were my beloved companions throughout my childhood. When I moved from the nursery school into the primary school, things went completely over my head. We had to stand as a class to recite the multiplication tables. I just mimed and no one ever seemed to notice. Although I was shy, I was one of the few girls prepared to play kissing games with the boys. I was aware of this contrast between the out-going aspects of my personality (my willingness to push myself to take risks) and my shy timidity throughout my life.

3

Trevor lived in a small studio room on the mezzanine floor. A pull-out double bed was folded up into a wall cupboard during the day. On the mantelpiece, there was a small ceramic Mrs. Tittlemouse from Beatrix Potter and on the floor, a large green bottle full of coloured marbles. I also noticed the small white marble statuette, a contoured nude of a young man in the Greek classical style. Trevor enjoyed showing me all the European countries and their capitals in his atlas. For the most part, he left us to amuse ourselves. We would draw or play with our teddies while he read the newspaper.

Trevor was tall and handsome. Now in his late forties, he had a protruding belly. His hair was receding and going grey. Trevor had an easy well-spoken charm and a high brow that gave him an intelligent appearance. He wore heavy scents and was often tanned from his travels. I was fascinated by his large hands, which I would hold and inspect. His nails were well-manicured. I always bit mine. Trevor liked to wear rings and, for many years, he wore a gold sovereign on a chain around his neck. He was fond of hugging us. He told us how affection had been lacking in his own childhood. I enjoyed his hugs but I found his tickling too excruciating to bear.

While he was living in Battersea, Trevor worked as a driver for a delivery service of imported flowers. He used to drive his mini-clubman van out to Heathrow airport where he collected boxes full of orchids. Occasionally he took us along with him. He had always been interested in travel and exotic destinations. He took us to the viewing area at Heathrow where he showed us the planes taking off and landing. Then we drove into central London where he used to deliver the orchids to hotels such as the Dorchester in Park Lane.

There were no seat belt laws then so Sarah and I sat on the floor in the back of the van looking out of the rear windows. To amuse ourselves we pretended that the small square windows were televisions. If we were feeling brave, we would wave to the driver of the vehicle behind. Trevor loved sweets of all kinds. Occasionally as a special treat, he took us a favourite patisserie of his in the West End. He ordered large white meringues with freshly whipped cream in the middle. The elegant and luxurious shop created a stark contrast to the drabness of the flat we lived in. Because of these comparisons, I grew up very conscious of social differences.

# Holidays with Trevor and day outings with Jo

For years, Trevor kept a caravan in an orchard in the Cotswolds near Chipping Norton. The orchard was part of the extended garden of an old and rambling stone thatched cottage. A white-haired old woman called Joey owned the property. There were plum trees in the orchard that buzzed with wasps in the summer. We enjoyed the novelty of eating fruit straight from the trees. Once I was stung by one of them and my eye swelled up so I couldn't see. One time, Trevor had a friend with him, so Sarah and I stayed in the house overnight. It was the first time we had seen a bidet in the bathroom and we wondered what it was for. We played with a set of nested Russian wooden dolls. I came across an old lyre and spent hours discovering how to pick out my favourite tunes on the strings.

Sarah and I played in the countryside without any adult supervision, returning to the caravan at mealtimes. We spent hours building dams across small streams, using stones, mud and tufts of grass to fill the gaps. Joey's son lived nearby with his wife and two boys who were a similar age to us. Sometimes they would come and join in our games. I learned to cycle on one of the boy's bikes. I practised on the road by freewheeling along until I crashed into the nettles.

One day we came across a small lake nearby. There was a large raft by the edge, made of wooden planks buoyed up with oil drums. We decided to get on board and the boys found a long pole to push us along. All of a sudden, as we were drifting towards the middle of the pond, the boys said that they couldn't feel the bottom of the lake. It was looking as if the raft might sink. Since none of us could swim, we were all frightened. But I confidently reassured Sarah that we were not going to die. I was convinced that I was intended to live. Luckily Trevor arrived looking for us and we got back to shore.

I always wanted to be a tomboy but never had the courage to be as adventurous as the others were. Whenever we climbed trees, I was always the one who could not get down. One time I got stuck and Trevor came to my rescue. Once on the ground, I nursed my wounded pride by going with him on an errand in the car. Another time the boys brought a packet of cigarettes, which they offered to share with us. We hid in the tool shed and I tried one puff. I collapsed in a fit of coughing, which was enough to put me off. Nevertheless, I was pleased to have experienced this adult activity.

The boys lived in a large red-brick house some miles away. We enjoyed playing on their garden swing, made of a plank of wood and rope. They had no indoor toilet. The toilets were in an outbuilding. Inside there was a bench with three holes in a row including a smaller one for children. We could not resist peering down into the cesspit despite the smell. When we stayed overnight, we had to use a large china chamber pot, called a potty, kept under the bed. I explained Sarah's head-banging habit to the boys. She put her hands behind her head and rocked her head from side to side when going to sleep. She also made a humming noise, which annoyed me. Jo told me that a doctor had said it was probably a sign of emotional insecurity. I tried it once but I could not see the attraction. I found it involved too much effort and made me dizzy.

After we had been living in Battersea for a while, Jo applied to the court for visitation rights. Every other Saturday, she used to come to take us out for the day. Daphne would get us ready and take us down to the front door. One time, I was ill and Daphne refused to allow Jo to come upstairs to see me. Sarah went alone and I had to stay in bed feeling very deprived of motherly love. Visiting days were difficult when the weather was bad. There was nowhere to go.

Jo gave me a Tiny Tears doll and a large baby doll she called Debbie. She was sentimental about dolls. Perhaps they reminded her of her own childhood that was also deprived of motherly love. Maybe they compensated her in some way for being separated from her own children. Eventually she asked us to give them back to her to keep. The boys had scribbled over the dolls with ballpoint pen and pushed their eyes in. Despite her lack of money, Jo took the doll Debbie to a toy hospital and paid to have her mended.

On one visiting day, it was fine weather and Jo took us to the park. She showed us two new dolls she had bought. Jo told us that she would keep them for us when we visited her. She named them Beverley and Sally, the names she had wanted to call us when we were born. Trevor had apparently chosen our names. He disliked the modern fashion of using nicknames so he chose names for us that couldn't be shortened. For a few weeks, Jo was lodging in a room of a private house in the suburbs of London and the couple allowed her to use their living room for the day. Sarah and I spent the afternoon playing with a red plastic tea set Jo had bought for us.

Early on Jo wrote reluctantly to her elder brother Arthur and asked him to put her up until she found a home. Jo had a proud nature and she found Arthur's lecturing impossible to take. In common with others, Arthur had liked Trevor. While my parents were married, Arthur and his wife were invited up to London to see a show with them. They ate together afterwards at Trevor's expense. To all appearances, Jo and Trevor were devoted to each other. When my parents separated, Arthur and his wife were among those who were surprised because Jo and Trevor had always seemed so well-suited. They were certainly both unconventional people.

Now Jo sat around her brother's house, chain-smoking and saying little. She moved on as soon as she could and found lodgings near Romford, in the suburbs of East London, which meant a long journey by tube on visiting days. When the underground train drew into the station, we had to run down the platform looking for a smoking compartment. We spent these long tedious journeys counting off the underground stations, which we came to know by heart. Years later Jo told me how a man once sat opposite us wearing only a raincoat. She spent the whole journey trying to keep us distracted so we wouldn't notice and comment on his genitals.

To pay for the train fare Jo took a job in a factory packing butter. One week she worked the 2pm to 10pm shift and the following week she did the 6am to 2pm shift. As she found the work very monotonous, Jo would take a word from the dictionary every day and see how many other words she could find in it. One of the foremen used to help her. Jo was going to a doctor at the time and she told him that she had changed from not being able to have anything to do with men to wanting anyone. He asked her what had been happening in her life. When she told him about losing custody of her children, he told her that it was most likely not men she wanted but a baby. He prescribed the contraceptive pill for her.

All went well for about six months and Jo thought it would be safe to stop taking the pill. But within a few weeks she was pregnant. The father was the foreman at work. There was not much chance that he would want to take the baby away from her. He already had twins and two other children. Jo felt she could not cope and asked the doctor if she could go into hospital for a while. She was given an interview with the head of Warley Hospital near Brentwood. It was agreed that she would stay at the mental hospital during the week and return to her flat at weekends so that she could see us.

When Jo was released from the mental hospital, the report said that she was suffering from a slight form of schizophrenia. The opinion was that if she was to have any more stress in her life it might lead to a psychotic breakdown. Jo's own view was that she was clinically depressed. She wore loose clothing when she came to see us and kept her pregnancy secret from us so that we would not tell Daphne. She did not want Trevor to know in case it stood against her in the lawsuit she was bringing against him to regain custody.

Jo had kept her married name after her divorce. She hated her maiden name, King, which she associated with poverty and shame. When her son was born in September 1967, she named him Simon Thomas Hare so that he had the same initials as Trevor. It was her way of getting back at Trevor who had always wanted a son. Jo still had nowhere to live and so it was agreed that foster parents should look after the baby initially. Jo returned to work at the factory and visited Simon one weekend and us the next. Our older sister Anne lived too far away so Jo only saw her once while living in Romford.

Jo applied to the local council for housing. For a long time, they refused to house her because she did not have enough points to be eligible for council housing. Finally, they agreed to give her a flat in Gidea Park and she applied to get Simon (now a toddler) back from his foster family. Simon's foster mother, Shirley, wrote a letter begging Jo to let them keep him. Shirley and Howard had five children of their own, plus two adopted and many fostered. They had a nice home in Essex and were no doubt concerned for his future growing up in the poverty of a council flat. But Jo was determined to finally succeed in raising this youngest child of hers.

Now that she had Simon living with her, Jo could no longer work to pay for tube fares. Her doctor asked her why she did not ask her rich brother Arthur to help. But Jo was too proud to ask her brother for money. The doctor replied that, if she did not ask him, then he would. So Jo wrote to Arthur who agreed to send £5 every other week to pay for a taxi to drive us from London for the weekend. I remember how self-conscious and privileged I felt during these silent, chauffeur-driven car rides. My mother's flat was in a modern high-rise block. The first day Sarah and I went up and down in the lift until someone complained. This was the first time that we stayed with Jo overnight since we had moved to Battersea.

The years in Gidea Park were difficult for Jo. She had very little money and spent months living on nothing but a loaf of bread for the week. She had almost no furniture so her flat was barren. Luckily Sarah and I were used to amusing ourselves. Jo and I played cards together for hours. Jo taught me the games she had learned as a child: rummy and brag, a gambling game that we used as practice for sorting cards. Sarah must have played with Simon. Sarah had always been a fussy eater and at mealtimes Jo would play aeroplanes or make up stories to encourage Sarah to eat. It was no doubt Sarah's way of getting the parental attention she was missing.

## Visiting my father's parents in Durham City

In his youth, Trevor had only gone home to get the money he needed. But once he had custody of us, he used Granny and Barbara, as family to babysit so that he was free to do what he wanted. He seemed to enjoy at least some of this contact. If nothing else, it meant he didn't have to cook. We were frequent travellers up and down the A1 or The Great North Road as Trevor called it. The journey from London to Durham was just under 300 miles and took around five hours. Carsickness was a problem for me until teenage years. Sarah and I played games to pass the time, like counting the number of cars of each colour. At one time I taught Sarah the alphabet. Trevor preferred the A1 dual carriageway to the newer M1 motorway. The road was quieter, with fewer large trucks and we could stop for lunch at one of the roadside pubs.

We grew to recognise the roundabouts at Stamford, Grantham and Doncaster as mileposts on our journey northwards. The huge chimneys of the power station at Ferrybridge heralded the North Country and by the time we reached Scotch Corner, our journey was almost over. Trevor explained how the road split at Scotch Corner. While we continued up the Eastern road, others joined the road that goes up the west coast of Scotland via Carlisle. My father had travelled this route ever since his childhood in the 1920s. In those days, it was more romantic: a single carriageway road with little traffic and quaint country inns ready to welcome travellers.

My grandparents had retired to a sprawling bungalow on the edge of Durham city. The Close was a new brick-built bungalow just above the city on Potters Bank. It had over an acre of garden and in summer Trevor spent many hours cutting the two large lawns. We saw little of him except at mealtimes. He kept himself busy all day long and so Granny looked after us. Sarah and I played in the garden on the paved areas. There was a fruit and vegetable garden outside the kitchen window and in summer, I enjoyed eating handfuls of raspberries and blackcurrants straight from the bushes.

Trevor had always been fascinated with trains. He admired the Swiss railways for their efficiency and cleanliness. When we were small, he kept a collection of electric toy trains in the annex of his parents' bungalow. We were not allowed to play with them because they were too expensive. He had built many different interlinking tracks so that he could run three or four different trains at the same time. He would buy new carriages and engines on his trips to Switzerland. Around this time, we also visited Betty Bailey who had been a childhood friend of Barbara and Trevor. Her father owned a chemist shop in Durham. Betty never married and later took over the shop from her father. She was now in her fifties. Trevor asked her to have us for a few hours now and then. Then one day, Trevor asked me how I would like to have Betty as a new mother. I liked Betty because she was nice to us. Not long after this, we stopped seeing her. I assume that he proposed and she turned him down.

Just inside the front door of the bungalow was a spacious hallway where we played. A grandfather clock in the hall produced an echoing ticking sound and an hourly chime. Once a week Grandpa wound up the clock with a special key. In the living room, a mantelpiece clock chimed the quarter hour. Sarah and I made up stories and played games with our teddies. We used blankets and cushions to build camps and homes out of chairs and side tables. My rabbit or bear was usually in charge and always telling Sarah's toys what to do. On winter mornings, Granny cleared and made up the coal fire in the lounge. We watched as she rolled up sheets of newspaper expertly, first into a long thin roll and then, bending the roll around her hand, into neat balls that she used to kindle the coal fire. In the evenings, she played solitaire with two packs of cards.

Grandpa was an enthusiastic soccer supporter. He let us help him fill in his football pools coupon and the newspaper 'Spot the ball' game. He smoked cigarettes with a filter holder and also cigars. The fragrant tobacco smells, the neatly made wooden boxes and the brightly coloured pipe cleaners fascinated us. Grandpa's hobby had been carpentry. Sarah and I were impressed by his garage, which had immaculate shelves of sets of wooden tool drawers. He had made doll's furniture for our cousin Sue. Sometimes Sarah and I walked with Grandpa into Durham along the river below the magnificent cathedral. As we passed through the shops, we asked him to buy us sweets or a small toy. Sometimes we were successful in persuading him and Granny would chastise him for spoiling us.

Granny had a home help, Frances, who did the housework and the ironing. Granny did the cooking herself and we often watched her in the kitchen, especially when she made cakes. We waited in hopeful anticipation for the mixing bowl and wooden spoons to lick at the end. She cooked traditional English food, meat with potatoes and vegetables. A favourite of ours was her chicken curry with sultanas and apple. We enjoyed the abundance of good food. I often had second helpings and even Sarah was less fussy than usual.

I particularly enjoyed Granny's puddings. One was a plain suet pudding, which she wrapped in a muslin cloth and steamed. It would roll out onto the serving dish looking unappetisingly grey. But it was very light and tasted delicious served with golden syrup. She also made real custard with milk and eggs cooked over a pan of simmering water. There was an open fire in the kitchen, which Granny used to grill lamb chops or beefsteaks as Grandpa liked them. Even breakfast was a formal set meal with kippers and a table laid with elegant porcelain dishes for the butter and the home-made marmalade. Every day, they used bone china crockery and silver cutlery with bone handles, which was kept in a wooden canteen.

Granny, now in her seventies, was always immaculately dressed. She explained to us how her rings had been given to her by Grandpa on various wedding anniversaries. She had smart travel luggage including a jewellery case. On her dressing table, I admired her matching set of ebony hairbrushes and a hand mirror all with her initial E for Elsie on the back of each piece. On our outings in their Rolls Royce motor car, my grandmother worn a hat and a fur stole around her neck. Oblivious to any concern for the dead animal, I was fond of stoking it, and fascinated with its legs and tail.

Grandpa wore a trilby hat and a three-piece suit. His pocket watch was attached to his waistcoat with a gold Albert chain. When we went out for a drive, Sarah and I sat in the back with Granny. My grandfather was always the driver. We enjoyed the luxurious feel of the wide leather seats and playing with the electric windows. My dearest childhood companions were my teddy bears so I was heart-broken when Granny insisted that I had to leave them at home. Sarah and I slept in a twin room next to my grandparent's bedroom. The beds were luxuriously soft and in the winter months, Granny switched on the electric blankets so the beds were warm by bedtime. Having a bath in the tiled bathroom with an accessories rack across the bath was a novelty. There was Pears soap and a real sponge. These are my only memories of bathing as a young child.

Like a schoolmistress, granny kept her distance with us. Her own upbringing had been Edwardian and no doubt equally strict. She believed that discipline was vital to raising well-behaved children. Granny never raised her voice. She used a reprimanding tone of voice or a firm squeeze of the hand with a stern look. Affection never came into her handling of children. Perhaps she was afraid that any emotional display would undermine her authority. My own parents often hugged and kissed us, so I thought her very unloving.

Once I left a toy out at the end of the garden. Granny asked me to fetch it, but I refused. I sat at the kitchen table stubbornly sulking for some time before I went to fetch the toy. I did not like to be reprimanded. Another time Granny asked us to wash our knickers in the washbasin. We were mystified but assumed that it was some form of punishment. It was her way of showing us that we needed to wipe our bottoms properly. As children, we didn't understand the subtle hint. Personally, I prefer a more straightforward approach. My parents were much more approachable. Trevor told me how he used to fart to keep the bed warm at boarding school.

Although the Hares were my father's family, I never felt we were accepted. At mealtimes, Granny asked politely after my mother. I never knew what she wanted to know. Even to a young child, it was obvious that my grandparents had a lifestyle that was more privileged than mine was ever likely to be. Their wealth, with its associated security and comfort, differentiated me from them. I resented Granny's strictness and disapproval. I was oblivious to the effects our cockney accents and unwashed bodies might have had. Later I appreciated that it was not her responsibility to care for us.

We were staying in the Cotswolds, in May 1969, when Trevor received a phone call telling him that Grandpa had been seriously injured in a traffic accident. My grandparents had been out shopping in the centre of Newcastle. As a bus swung past, Frank was somehow dragged under the wheels. The bones in both of his legs were badly broken. Despite the commotion, Granny had had the presence of mind to note the registration plate of the bus before it disappeared into the traffic. They received financial compensation from the bus company but my grandfather's active life was over. The surgeons tried to save his leg. But by this time Grandpa was in his early eighties and the bone would not mend. He had to have his leg amputated later that year. Frank Hare had spent his life on the other side of the hospital bed as a doctor and he made a very poor patient. He moved back home where Granny looked after him until he died in November 1971 aged 85 years.

## A privileged education in the North of England

In September 1969 Sarah and I arrived for our first term at boarding school in the North of England. I was eight and Sarah was just six years old. The Sneep was a private girls' school situated on a residential lane up the hill from the old market town of Hexham, Northumberland. Halfway along Hadrian's Wall, Hexham is surrounded by the history of the Romans in Britain. On Sundays, we were escorted into town in a column of pairs for a service in the historic abbey. This was the only time that we went into Hexham.

My cousin Sue had just left the school the previous summer. So the Sneep was a natural choice. It never occurred to me to feel homesick. We didn't have a home to miss and by this time we were used to living apart from our parents. The school was run on routine. Even though we lived in an institution, we had better care at school than we had had with Daphne. There were ten or so girls who boarded full-time, many more weekly boarders who went home at the weekend as well as day girls and boys. The boys left for their prep schools when they were 7 years old. Initially the other girls remarked on our cockney accents but we quickly lost them.

Sarah and I were put in in a dormitory with two other girls. One of these was Feri who became my best friend throughout The Sneep. Feri was amazed when I told her that I had never heard of the Bible. No one had taken us to church or read us stories from the Bible. Like me, Feri was quiet but she was a tomboy. Feri was fiercely proud of having short hair. She was close to her father and proudly showed me the Swiss army knife he had given her. I was never very macho and much more interested in my teddy bears. Feri had spent holidays with her young uncle, who was an expert in Victorian engineering. She like to help him while he worked on old steam traction engines. So by the time she was eight, Feri had already decided that she wanted to be a mechanical engineer.

My teddy bears were my family. I had a favourite daydream that one of my bears would come to life. With a live bear as a companion, I contemplated how popular I would be. Everyone would want to know me. Most of the free time I had at school, when we were not playing outside, I spent reading. The school library offered a wide selection of books including all the classics. We were given small notebooks to record the books we read during the term. Feri and I competed over who had the longest reading list by the end of term. I particularly enjoyed novels with an historical setting.

At first, I struggled with the class work. I had never learned to listen in class. With the smaller class sizes, I was noticed. I couldn't ignore the teacher as I had before. I still did not know my times tables and continued to cheat in tests. We were told to mark our own work and I simply made up the ticks and crosses. At the end of the first term, Feri was moved up to the next grade. I remained in the lower class, which was inconvenient for our out-of-school playtime as the two classes finished at different times. The following term I too was moved up. Initially I found the new class difficult. In English, they were reading 'The Water Babies' by Charles Kingsley. It is an old-fashioned, moral tale about a boy who is a chimney sweep. It was way over my head as a nine-year-old. I found the formal language of this English classic of 1863 quite unintelligible. Over time though, I became more involved in the classwork and learned how to respond to the education process. Eventually I caught up with the others. I became an attentive pupil and really enjoyed learning.

In lessons, we took turns to read from a textbook. Once a passage had been read, the books were turned over. The teacher would select one girl at random who was asked to summarise what we had just read. The prospect of being chastised in front of the whole class for not listening, provided an incentive for everyone to pay attention. In this new class, we had end of term exams. Mothers, who lived locally, volunteered to come into the school to assist. The pupils took turns to go to the dining room where we dictated our exam answers to one of the mothers. They wrote down our answers word for word. Even as we progressed higher up the school we never needed to revise for exams. This learning technique of listening and repeating ensured that we remembered the lessons.

Each term we studied one of Shakespeare's plays. My first play was 'A Midsummer Night's Dream' and I found it difficult to understand the meaning of the archaic poetry. Gradually though I found that, once the story had been explained, it could be quite enjoyable waiting to find out how some of the stories would end. We read 'Pilgrim's Progress' by John Bunyan together as a class and I enjoyed the story despite having little understanding of the religious significance. We learned about Roman history and culture as well as Latin. There were school trips to Hadrian's Wall and the local ruins of ancient Roman army camp and towns. I enjoyed the book 'From Ur to Rome', which gave an account of some of the earliest civilisations including those in Mesopotamia, Egypt and Greece. We also read the 'Tales of Troy' following the Greek hero, Ulysses in his tortuous quest of rescuing Helen from King Priam.

Each term we had to learn some passages by heart: one from the bible, one from Shakespeare and a poem. I enjoyed Portia's plea for mercy in 'The Merchant of Venice', the description of the night-time preparations for the Battle of Agincourt in 'Henry V' and Mark Anthony's speech inciting the crowd to take revenge for Brutus's murder of the emperor in 'Julius Caesar'. We learned these passages by testing each other. As usual Feri and I competed over who could get the best mark. We usually both got A+ but on one occasion when I was reciting to Mrs Herring, I was distracted by my surroundings and lost my way. It was a lovely sunny day and we were sitting out on the lawn beneath the copper beach tree.

'The Bat' by D H Lawrence described the author's sighting of a bat at dusk by the 'Ponte Vecchio' (The Old Bridge) in Florence: *"Bats! Creatures that hang themselves up like an old rag to sleep; And disgustingly upside down."* I had never imagined that I could enjoy poetry. Learning by heart, helped me appreciate how language can be used to express sentiments such as solitude, majesty and awe. As an adult, I have appreciated remembering some of the most poignant passages in the English language. Years later I used to commute to London Waterloo. While crossing the bridge, I enjoyed remembering the words of William Wordsworth: *"Earth hath not anything to show more fair! Dull would he be of soul who could pass by a sight so touching in its majesty."*

A private education allows adults to provide a greater level of attention to each child. Although I still felt deprived of a family home and contact with my mother, I had more of a sense that I was valued. I enjoyed the positive feedback of being one of the more able students. I felt that I belonged in an intellectual sense. But there was never any affection or emotion expressed. I often felt that Matron considered us a nuisance. I discovered the fantasy world of books, which provided an escape. Through books I could identify with the writer and share the feelings of the fictional characters. I enjoyed stories of other peoples' lives and experiences. It was interesting to compare differences and similarities. I now came to understand that other children had parents who were separated.

My school friends came from middle class families who lived in large houses and had a good lifestyle. I was often shocked by how disrespectful some of the girls were towards their parents. I could not imagine having the nerve to speak to my grandmother in that way and I was too fond of my parents to be rude to them. The parents were well-educated and the children had their own rooms, often with horses and stables. Neither Feri nor I had ever ridden a horse so we were bored by the other girls' constant talk of horses.

The school term was broken first by a quarter weekend, then a half-term week and finally a three-quarter weekend. Given the distance from our parents' homes, we spent these short breaks either with Granny or with friends. Sarah and I were often guests in other people's houses. I was always terribly shy when I stayed with a friend. They were more confident than I was and later knew about boys and pop music. During a birthday party at a girl's home, I had a short ride on a pony. It was a treat, like the donkey ride Trevor took us on once on Scarborough beach. Another mother devised a treasure hunt that involved us roaming all over the countryside trying to find and solve clues she had left. I was impressed and amazed that anyone would go to so much trouble for a birthday.

The most significant contact we had at school was Feri's family who lived in Scotland. Feri was the eldest of seven children. Feri's mother, Sari, had studied theology at Oxford and was an official in a Scottish Church. She ran residential courses for clergy. Sari was often busy with her Church duties in addition to having a big house to run. She was pleased to have Sarah and I as playmates for her children. The arrangement suited both sides well. Occasionally we reciprocated and had their daughters to stay at Granny's house. But there was much less to do and Granny did not have any transport. We had to go to my Aunt Barbara's house for entertainment.

Feri's family lived in a large mansion on a country estate near Edinburgh. The family owned a major European transport and logistics company, also formally shipping interests. When I first went to their house as a child, I found the place awe-inspiring because it was so grand and massive. This was a different world for me where it was possible to get lost just looking for the bathroom. Feri's parents, Sari and Robin, were always welcoming and evidently pleased that their children had made friends. The fact that we were not from a wealthy or well-connected family never seemed to be an issue. Meals were prepared for us and occasionally we went on outings. For the most part, the time we spent was unsupervised.

Feri's younger siblings were looked after by a nanny. The older children lived in a more independent world. We roamed about the house or the grounds making our own entertainment as we always did. We played near the stream that ran through the grounds past the walled vegetable garden. We cleared sticks from the river or made a path through the garlic smelling plants that covered our Italia Island. We built camps and planned adventures. For one birthday, Feri was given a canoe, which she rowed down the river. I was never remotely interesting in trying it. I didn't want to get cold and wet. The house was full of books. Feri's mother was an avid reader and there were many books from her childhood. So if the weather was bad, we would read. In the basement playroom there was a large wooden rocking horse that a small child could ride on.

## Boarding school indoor fun and outdoor games

In the spring of 1972, industrial action meant there were regular power cuts. We had fun with candles in the bathroom and dormitories. Feri and I were the only full boarders in our year, so at weekends we had the dormitory to ourselves. In the week, immediately the lights were turned off, we enjoyed slipping out of bed before the other girls' eyes had grown used to the darkness. Then we could keep everyone else in suspense wondering where we were hiding ready to pounce on the unsuspecting. Occasionally someone started a pillow fight. Either matron or a teacher was always on duty so we couldn't make too much noise before we were caught. When I was ten, I was hit from behind during a fight and I broke one of my front teeth on the metal bar at the end of the bed.

Life at school revolved around routine, lessons and our free time spent playing outdoors. In the morning, there was a first bell followed by a second bell five minutes later. We had to lay out our socks and knickers out on a chair before we went to bed at night. Even our knickers were uniform, both the blue knickers and the larger brown ones that were worn over the blue pair. Mufti (non-uniform clothes) was also prescribed and included slacks, as my grandmother used to refer to women's trousers, and a tartan kilt.

As we were growing up our friendships became a focal point for our conversations and our playtime. In my diary, I used to say exactly what I thought so some entries were not very charitable. In living together, we were more like sisters than friends and everything was discussed. We sat around talking about the more difficult girls. Laura had a strong personality and she was often in trouble with the rest of us. Laura was more socially mature and in touch with the world than Feri and me. Laura was a weekly boarder and she had a close relationship with her mother who provided insights into life outside school. In our senior years Laura told us about the mysterious objects she found in her mother's drawers.

Possessiveness and jealousy occurred frequently. One of my early difficulties in my relationships with friends was my pride and my consequent reluctance to explain my own behaviour. I was distant with Laura when I was cross with her but, because of personal pride, I was too embarrassed to say why. I never had this problem with Feri who was less socially adventurous and so perhaps more loyal to our friendship. I found that I enjoyed having friendships with different people. But Laura made friends easily and I was offended when she preferred one of her other friends over me.

On birthdays, the birthday girl was given the bumps by her dorm. Everyone grabs an arm or a leg and together they lift you up in the air as they count the number of years. I was woken on a Sunday for my bumps one whole hour before the morning bell was due to sound. For my eleventh birthday Trevor sent me a jewellery box covered in black leather that played music. I used this box to store my miniature bottle of French perfume, an embroidered silk handkerchief and other sentimental objects (all from Trevor).

On the last night of term there was a tradition of giving everyone apple-pie beds. We would untuck the bottom sheet and fold it up and over the top sheet. When the victim gets into bed, they cannot get their feet further than a foot or two into the bed. It was an effective way of giving someone a surprise until they realised what had happened. At the end of term, we had a midnight feast. The weekly boarders smuggled in cake and biscuits, which we hid until the last night. I confided in my diary *"Last days of term are lovely."*

Over the years Feri and I, as full-time boarders, had time to develop more involved games. The most sophisticated of these was called 'Hares and Rabbits' after my surname Hare. I was a March hare because of my birthday. Feri was a mountain rabbit as she came from Scotland. Over time many of the other girls wanted to join in our game. So we evolved a whole series of tests and procedures that a new girl had to be tested on if she wanted to qualify to join in.

There was a hierarchy and naturally Feri and I were at the most senior levels of the game. The other girls had to learn our rules to achieve this level of privilege. I enjoyed the control and being in charge. Most of the game was about establishing and maintaining a camp as well as making our own brooms and building mock fires. It was our way of mimicking the outdoor activities we read about in books such as Arthur Ransome's 'Swallows and Amazons'. Feri was the practical one whereas I was more domesticated, taking the lead in camp making. Feri used her pen knife to shape bows and arrows.

The head teacher, Miss McConchie had a small flat on the first floor in an annex beyond the assembly hall. On winter weekends, she invited the full boarders to her sitting room. We sat on the rug in front of her fire doing a piece of needlework and listened while she read a chapter from a book. Miss McConchie always chose thought-provoking books and was talented in using her voice to make the stories come alive. There was a television in the assembly hall and in winter we were allowed to watch a couple of programmes on Saturday afternoons. There was Cilla Black's show as well as various children's serials such as Pollyanna, Anne of Green Gables and Walt Disney's Wonderful World of Colour.

School terms lasted ten weeks or more. Time at school was divided into lessons, meals and play time outdoors. At weekends Miss McConchie or matron was on duty. After lunch on Saturday whoever was on duty took us on a long walk outside the school grounds. One of my favourite destinations was the woods, which we walked to via the lane above the school. In the woods, we built wigwams out of the fallen branches of fir trees. Other times we took the bus to a nearby lake where we tried to reach the small islands.

We walked along country lanes lined with cow parsley, yarrow, campions and foxgloves. The woods smelled of bracken and in the late spring, the woods were carpeted with bluebells. Other common flowers were white and red dead nettles, speedwell and forget-me-nots. Walking across the moors and open ground we passed gorse and broom bushes as well as many varieties of heather. These walks contributed to my later enjoyment of walking in the countryside.

Miss McConchie told us about the different wild plants along the way. She explained that every plant belongs to a family. One of these were vetches, which are like a small wild sweet pea. More unusual sightings were Lords and ladies (cuckoo pint), bulrushes and stinking hellebore. Thistles and various varieties of knapweed were more ordinary. We learned to differentiate between a buttercup and a celandine, a primrose and a cowslip. We learned that chickweed, bindweed and groundsel are just weeds. Once we found a bright orange disc-shaped fungus called Ladies' fingers growing on a tree. Every week in our nature lessons, we painted a plant from our walk, describing where we had found it. Miss McConchie also pointed out the calls of the common wild birds.

Every day we were sent outside to play. Only if it was raining heavily could we stay indoors where we sat on the desks in one of the classrooms. Just below the tennis courts and above the field, there was a row of small plots. We full boarders adopted one of these each as our own and grew flowers or vegetables, like broad beans, which we didn't like to eat but they were quick to grow. The winters were cold and each year there was snow and ice on the ground for a few weeks. We flattened the snow to make a slide. The first signs of spring came with the snowdrops and daffodils, closely followed by the attractive bushes of Pussy Willow with their long flowing catkins and furry buds. The school overlooked sloping grounds covering a few acres. The grounds included a large garden with formal lawns and rose gardens, which were off bounds to children.

The main garden consisted of open ground and paths where we played. We built camps or played hide-and-seek games in the holly and hawthorn bushes. There were also copses of trees, including hazel and crab apple. We spent hours collecting items from the garden. In autumn, there were acorns and conkers. We ate the beechnuts from the copper beach tree. We collected the fallen leaves from the trees in large piles and then kicked our way through them for the fun of seeing the leaves all tossed about. In the more formal areas of the garden, there were snowberry bushes with their attractive but poisonous white balls, which we squished under foot to see their contents of clear liquid burst out. There were dog roses and rose hips. Honesty was an attractive plant with its old-penny-shaped transparent seed pods. In summer the lilac bushes, with their clusters of white and purple flowers, had an evocative scent.

The younger children played towards the top of the garden where there was a sandpit and swings. We used to play hopscotch, marking out our own squares on the ground. For many months in the winter, we played French skipping with a long piece of elastic. Two girls stood inside the circle of elastic to hold it in place at ankle, knee or hip height. The third player had to jump in and out of the circle, taking the elastic with her feet, in a prescribed set of moves to complete the game. Of course, there was always tag and the inevitable horse games. The girl pretending to be the horse wore a skipping rope over her shoulders so that she could be steered from behind. Then someone else, pretending to be the rider, would pull on the rope and give instructions such as gee up and halt. It is interesting that girls engage in play involving control in this way. Compared with boys, who are more energetic and perhaps combative in their play (running around with sticks and hitting each other), girls seem to be more orderly and structured in their play.

There was a field of mown grass on the lower slopes, which was used on sports day. At the bottom of the field, a couple of copses of silver birch trees were surrounded by longer grass. In the summer, we played on the bars. There were two sets of bars, a small set for the juniors at the bottom of the field and a larger set for the older girls at the top. It was possible to do a full turn or somersault over the top bar and continue to do a further turn around the lower bar onto the ground. Handstand competitions were also popular and we played 'Sun, rain, thunder, lightning' for hours on end.

Halfway down the hill, just above the field, was a tennis court, which doubled as a netball pitch. On the far side of the garden beyond the tennis courts, there was a sport's hut where we had our lessons in gymnastics, ballet and Scottish country dancing. We also had Brownies. I never enjoyed ball games. Netball bored me and I never saw the point in chasing around after a ball. One day I questioned why I should even pretend to be interested in the whereabouts of the ball. I stopped dodging about and just stood on the pitch watching the others. The games teacher spotted me and sent me into the school building to be reprimanded by the head mistress. I had to accept that sport was a compulsory activity at boarding school regardless of my inclination or ability. Trevor reassured me that he had always hated sport when he was at school.

## Coping with discipline and standing up to authority

Trevor had been unhappy when he went away to boarding school. Jo said that when they were married, he swore that he would never send us away to board. Naturally his circumstances changed with their divorce. Trevor still wanted to be reassured that we were happy at school. He said how glad he was that we did not cry when we went back to school. In part, we had no sense of having a home to miss. Later, his pride in our apparent indifference to returning to school ensured that we tried to hide any emotion we did feel.

There was little concept of what boarding schools now refer to as pastoral care. We were never offered a hug or an inquiry as to our happiness. Discipline was strict but there was rarely cause for more than a stern word. I was a timid child and I was embarrassed by how easily I got upset whenever I was in trouble. I often thought that others should make excuses for me because my parents were so distant. Once when some other girls were caught out of their dormitories Miss McConchie administered the slipper. This was not a serious corporal punishment but only intended to shame the wrongdoers. When we were seniors, a girl was caught swearing. Mrs Herring gave us all a lecture about the evils of swearing and told us we would be expelled for swearing. We decided to be careful about saying 'bloody', which was probably the worst word we ever used.

On parents' days Feri's mother, knowing we had no one else to see, looked out for Sarah's and my artwork. There were other times when we felt a lack of parental interest and support. On winter mornings, matron gave out orange vitamin tablets that many parents provided for their daughters. As far as we were concerned these pills were just sweets. One of the daygirls offered to buy some for Sarah and me. The next thing I knew was that Mrs Herring wanted to see me. Sarah had eaten the whole packet. I thought it unjust to be told off when I had not eaten a single one! I was often held responsible for my sister. Sarah was a pretty fair-haired child, who gained attention for being younger. Her shyness made it difficult for adults, even our parents, to know how to interact with her and she would be babied where I never was. I learned to be more self-sufficient while Sarah took shelter from the world behind me.

Many of the books we read at school did not come from the school library. Enid Blyton's books, although a little dated, were all read avidly. I enjoyed her books because she used easy words. The school did not approve of this lack of vocabulary. Some of the weekly boarders brought her books into school and so we full boarders were able to read them. Naturally, we read her stories set in boarding schools. These fictional girls had much more fun and adventure than we ever did. I envied the heroine in Malory Towers for having thoroughly respectable, middle-class married parents.

As soon as the second bell rang in the morning, the race was on to line up at the door, dressed in our dressing gowns and underwear. We waited in turn for matron to tell us to go to the bathroom with a flannel and hand towel. After breakfast, we queued again outside the two upstairs toilets. Matron kept a register to check for constipation and we reported whether we had 'been' or 'not been'. Amongst ourselves, we talked about number 1 and number 2. In the evening, we bathed in groups of four with two girls in the bath at a time. It was Laura who told me that we should wash between our legs. We washed our hair over a basin once every three weeks.

Food was a constant source of pleasure and dread. Fried bread for breakfast was one of my favourites. Most Fridays I would write *"Fish – yuk!"* in my diary. The white flavourless boiled cod used to stink out the dining room. A regular exception to the white fish was a bright yellow smoked haddock that was almost as bad. Lunch was usually roast meat with potatoes and other vegetables. Thursdays meant Irish stew and tapioca for pudding. Both were favourites of mine and I used to eat everyone else's tapioca, which was not popular for its consistency. There were no snacks between meals so by mealtimes I was hungry. Despite being skinny, I was always a healthy eater. As a cooking demonstration Mrs Herring showed the older girls how to make a simple pudding: bread soaked in hot milk and cinnamon. It made me feel sick and it was the only dish I could never eat. Nevertheless, Mrs Herring insisted that I had to sit at the table facing my serving until teatime. But I never ate the pudding.

The school was the home of the headmistress, Mrs Herring, and her husband. In summer, they used to invite friends to the house to play tennis. They had a grown-up son, who visited from time to time and ate with us. In the summer months, there were always impressive displays of fresh flowers in the main hallway of the school. Mrs Herring was evidently amused by my fascination as I watched her create a structure and colour balance with flowers collected from the school's formal gardens. She was a handsome woman and kept her dark shoulder-length hair fastened back in a large hair slide. She dressed elegantly in colour co-ordinated tweeds with matching expensive-looking low-heeled shoes. She was Swiss by birth and our main interaction with her came through French classes in the senior years. She was a figure of authority and we were intimidated by her. She rarely displayed any humour or affection.

We learned the school vernacular on arrival. Mrs Herring's nickname was inevitably Kipper. I did not even dare write Mrs Herring's nickname in my diary in case she found it. Miss McConchie was more affectionately called Conkers. She was an educated spinster with a sharp tongue. We were not allowed any thoughtlessness or sloppiness. I was always nervous of being reprimanded for some transgression of speech or action. Miss McConchie was strict but she softened a little and showed more warmth as we progressed through the school. She was the form mistress of the senior girls and we came to respect and like her.

As juniors, our conversation among ourselves at mealtimes consisted of telling jokes. But if we sat next to an adult then we were expected to make proper conversation. I never knew what to say but shyness was not an excuse. Miss McConchie would often take me aside and give me a lecture about how boring and selfish it was to have nothing to say. As an adult, I have come to understand this perspective. As a child I could not think of any natural topic of conversation to discuss with adults. Other girls went home for the weekend so at least they could talk about what they had done outside school. The teachers already knew my weekend activities.

In my senior years, when we were expected to be more conversational at the table, I dreaded having to talk to Miss McConchie. If she thought that I was avoiding sitting beside her, she would move me next to her. This action was not a good precursor to making relaxed conversation. Ultimately, I found a coping strategy, which was to choose to sit next to her at a time when I felt there would be least pressure on me. I decided that this was mostly likely to be Monday breakfast. All week I agonised over suitable topics and then the night before, lying awake in bed I would rehearse. As long as I had two or three sentences, I could hope to satisfy the requirement that I had made an effort at conversation. Once this meal was over, I could relax. Having done my duty, I knew I would not need to sit next to a teacher for another week.

One of the most frightening events at the Sneep was the annual flu injection, which most pupils had each autumn. The first year was fine. But the second year I was affected by the atmosphere of tension and tears among the girls. Our names were called out one at a time. We waited our turn in a long line down the stairs from the bedrooms where a team of nurses were giving the injections. They used staple guns that made a loud punching noise. Watching girls coming back down the stairs in tears with blood dripping down their arm filled me with panic. I started to move back in the line.

Mrs Herrings spotted this and took a firm hold of my arm, moving me towards the front of the queue. Just before the nurse could give me the injection, I jerked my arm away and pushed against the headmistress. There was a commotion and I was put into one of the dormitories to calm down. I sat there for some time planning my escape and feeling victimized. Mrs Herring appeared and told me I was being childish. She told me to choose between a smack or the injection. I was aware of sounding pathetic but the decision was easy. I asked for the smack. Despite the rebuke, I was relieved to have avoided the injection. A senior girl told me I should have been ashamed of my behaviour. Many people conform to society's rules because they are unwilling to incur the bad opinion of others. But I like to make my own choices. I do not like to be bullied.

Throughout the following year, I dreaded the next flu jab. I had tried to impress on Trevor how much I did not want to have this injection but I was not confident that he would take the necessary action. When the time came the following autumn, I listened attentively with heart banging and was relieved when I did not hear my name read out. But I had missed my name and the head teacher marched me up the stairs to have the injection. The nurse was particularly sensitive in administering it, so I lived. Later Trevor saw a TV programme linking injections with mentally backward children and he resolved that we should have no more injections.

When we were ten, one of the girls had her first period and Mrs Herring gave us a book about the so-called facts of life. It described the basic reproductive biology with no hint of eroticism or romance. I remember being quite incredulous that the adults I saw around me would ever engage in such crude activity. Needless to say, there was never any follow-up session to allow us to ask questions. No one ever made any comment on the topic. When we were eleven Laura, Kirsten and Sally came back to school with bras. They stood around talking about bras, boys and pop music. None of this conversation focused on eroticism or sex itself. It revolved around the romantic implications of young girls hoping for male admiration. Feri and I had little interest in such things as we had no chance of experiencing them. We continued with our childish but more imaginative games. Despite living together in such close proximity with other girls, there was never a hint of any overt sexual activity so I am bemused by stories of little girls who masturbate.

# PART II: MY MOTHER'S FAMILY

## The poverty and deprivations of the King family

As I was reaching my pre-teens, Jo started telling me stories about her childhood. I found them fascinating. The information came here and there in occasional conversations and casual comments. Many years later my mother and her brother, Arthur, gave me a more detailed account of their childhood and the King family.

My grandfather, Ernest King was born sometime around 1908. He was a traveller or as they were sometimes called in those days, a Didicoy: people descended from Irish tinkers. When we were small Jo used to call us chavvy, which she told us meant child in traveller language. Ernest married a georgie, a non-traveller, called Gwendoline Minnie Rance. They had four children: Arthur was born in 1935, my mother Joan in 1938 and Tommy in 1940. There was also a younger daughter Maureen but she died. The couple often had violent fights and the children learned to get out of the way quickly. Gwendoline was known to throw pans, complete with their contents, across the room at Ernest. Even as a young child Jo was frightened and embarrassed by her mother's erratic behaviour.

When Jo was six, Gwendoline was forcibly removed from their home, screaming. She spent the rest of her life in a mental hospital. This unpleasant scene was naturally upsetting for the children. But no one ever explained their mother's sudden and traumatic departure because of the taboo over mental illness. Gwendoline had spent time in mental hospital before and Ernest's mother had to look after the children. Gran was widowed and, as there were no old folks' homes in those days, she lived with her son's family.

When Gwendoline came back home on the former occasion, one of the teachers at school was able to deduce that she was back because of the deterioration in the children's cleanliness. Almost twenty years later, Arthur received a letter from a mental hospital informing him that his mother was dying of stomach cancer. Together with Jo and Tommy, he visited Gwendoline just two days before she died in 1963. Arthur was surprised to find her quite lucid and not at all mad as he had expected. Amazingly Gwendoline still had a clear memory of their lives together all those years ago.

World War II had just ended. Ernest had to find work. With their mother gone, he needed to find someone to look after the children. Gran was getting too old and there were no other relatives willing to take them on. So Ernest took Jo, aged seven, and Tommy, aged four, to an orphanage in Esher, Surrey. Years later, Jo wrote:

"When we arrived, the staff covered us in a blue liquid. This I understand was to get rid of the fleas and scabies. Then we were given night clothes, which I had never seen before so I had to ask the staff what I was supposed to do with them. After my father left, Tommy and I sat on a seesaw and I cried. Tommy put his arms around me and told me not to cry because he was going to look after me. Tommy was to get one beating while we were there and that was because he found a hole in the floorboards over the staff dining room and urinated down it and got others to do the same.

Once he did it when they were eating; that is when he got the beating. I was beaten because one day when most of the staff and other children were out for the day, I climbed an old Magnolia tree in the grounds, which we had been forbidden to do. The teacher Miss Carpenter beat me with a bamboo stick all over my body. Tommy was caught as well but he was just sent to bed. He heard me crying in the dormitory and came to see what was wrong.

I stood up and pulled my nightgown up and showed him my body. It had large wheals all over it. We went to church, which I did not mind at all but I hated the dresses we had to wear. They were made of some sack-like cloth and were very rough. We were given 4 pennies to spend at the home's tuck shop a week. If you did anything wrong or your clothes got torn, they took some away and I remember being quite put out because I had some money taken from me when my apron was returned from the laundry ripped and I was convinced that I was not responsible."

Ernest rarely visited. One time he brought Arthur who spent the visit playing cricket with a boy he met. Afterwards Arthur could not understand why his father told him off for not spending any time with his younger brother and sister. Arthur was sent to board at The

Shaftsbury Boys' School at Bisley but after three months they expelled him for repeatedly running away. Arthur joined his father who was working as a farm labourer in Alton, Hampshire. Together they lived in a tent, constructed from a framework of hazel poles with a heavy tarpaulin stretched over them. To start with, Gran was living elsewhere so the ten-year-old Arthur had to cook the meals.

Due to the extensive German bombing in the south of England, there was a severe housing shortage after the war. The poor had nowhere to live. Ernest had heard about an abandoned army camp on the Duke of Wellington's estate at Heckfield, in Hampshire. So father and son set off to investigate. The camp was a collection of military style Nissen huts made of corrugated steel sheets. Other people were writing their names on the huts so that they could return later to claim their accommodation. They were breaking down doors to put their belongings inside and take possession. Following suit, Ernest wrote 'Taken by E. King' on one of the huts.

Having no crockery, they drank tea out of jam jars. Furniture was made from whatever they could find lying around the camp. They turned metal bomb-holders upside down and used them as chairs. They made beds out of steel strips and filled sacks with bracken and straw to make mattresses. Everyone got lousy very quickly. Round combustion stoves, left behind by the army, provided the hut's heating. Gran came to live with them. She had never worn a bra and her long, thin breasts stretched halfway down her body. Gran had breast cancer but, believing that her time had come, she refused to have an operation. The cancer caused her breast to burst and Gran used to swab the open wound with pieces of torn cloth that she would then throw onto the fire. Living in such primitive conditions and in close proximity, there was little personal privacy.

Ernest started courting a woman who lived on the other side of the camp. The couple used Arthur as a messenger, who deciphered his father's sign-off: IWALY (I will always love you). Bet Wyeth had four children of her own: Jean born in 1937, Graham in 1941, Doreen 1942 and David 1943. With someone to take care of them, Jo and Tommy returned home. The family moved to Bet's hut leaving Gran on her own. The older children resented their stepmother because she favoured her own children. At first, they called her Aunt Bet but Ernest insisted they had to call her Mum.

Bet and Ernest had another four children together: Maureen in 1947, Johnnie in 1948, Robert in 1949 and Margaret in 1954. As a child, I was curious to see Jo's step- and half-siblings but she had little contact with her family so we never knew them. The older girls had to look after the younger ones. On Sundays, lunch was always at 3pm after the pubs shut. After lunch, Ernest and Bet would go to bed and the children were sent outside to play. Jo's happiest childhood memories were of the time she spent playing with her brothers and sisters in the fields and countryside around Heckfield.

Eventually their living conditions improved slightly when the council put two huts together to provide three separate sleeping areas. Ernest and Bet slept in one room, the boys in another and the girls in the third. Each room had only one bed so the children had to sleep together. Jo described the appalling conditions in which they all lived: *"In the tin hut where we lived there was no hot water. So, a wash for the day was a dab of cold water on our face in the morning. I slept in a bed with two babies in it who were not potty trained so you can imagine how the rest of us stank.*

*The mattress was not changed until there were maggots crawling from it. We had fleas in our hair, clothes and stuck to our bodies. Not surprisingly the general public did not take kindly to us. Once a week we got a bath. A small tin bath was put on an open fire outside (weather permitting) and then transferred to a large one in the house. The smallest had a bath first, then the next, until it got to us older ones. By that time the water was so filthy that we must have come out dirtier than we went in."*

Jo dwelt on the deprivation, both social and emotional. Arthur was much more inclined to see the lighter side of their childhood. One time they were in Aldershot when Bet pointed to a pair of shoes that were on display outside a shop. She told Arthur and Tommy that she wanted them. The two boys had to grab the shoes and just run for it. They saw it all as a bit of a prank. As a boy, Arthur loved to go carol singing because they were given money. In 1948 one couple invited them in and they saw a television for the first time.

Bet insisted that they all had to steal from the local shops, which Jo resented: *"Bet was as evil as my mother was mad. She used her children to steal and when I came on the scene they no longer had to, I did. If I refused, I got what I called the cold treatment from Bet and her eldest daughter Jean. The atmosphere in a room would be so thick that one felt you could cut it with a knife. It made me feel very lonely and uncared for. In time, I would give in and steal what they wanted but not always. We had to go carol singing every year to make money for Christmas, so they told us. It did not stop Bet from making me steal everything on the Christmas tree. For years, I could not stand the sight of a Christmas tree."*

The only chance the children had to go to the seaside was the Sunday School's annual trip to Hayling Island. So once a week they went to a Church Sunday school, called Sunshine Corner, held in a hut on Heckfield Common. Arthur remembered the song they were taught for the rest of his life: *"Sunshine Corner, oh it's jolly fine. It's for children under ninety-nine. All are welcome; seats are given free. Sunshine corner: it's the place for me!"*

## The King children miss school to work in the fields

There was not much choice about stealing because the family had to eat. Ernest told Arthur that the only thing he needed to worry about was getting caught. Each spring Arthur helped his father pick all the daffodils from the grounds of Stratfield Saye House, which they sold to a greengrocer in Camberley. Arthur chuckled later at the thought that the Duke of Wellington never got to see his daffodils bloom! Another risky business was rabbit poaching for which they used ferrets and nets. Arthur was caught once on the Wellington Estate at Stratfield Saye and fined 10 shillings. Ernest also collected spare lead from around the camp, which after melting down into unidentifiable ingots, he sold to raise money for the family. From these experiences Arthur concluded that those with money never experience the strength of the survival instinct. He decided that it was easy for the rich to be moral, which I agree is probably true. Principles and morals are a luxury of the rich.

Ernest worked for many different employers over time. One of his employers was a farmer called Mr Bucknell at Stratfield Saye, who rented his farmland from the Duke of Wellington's estate. It was in the farmers' interests to keep the labourers employed to stop them drifting away to find work elsewhere. So there were often jobs around. In winter, there was hedging and ditching work. One winter when he was fourteen Arthur missed school from January until Easter. Every spring the family moved back to Alton to live in tents.

During the summer months, the children worked in the fields helping their father with hoeing, pulling mangles (large swedes grown to feed cattle) and pea-picking. Ernest passed quickly down a row of plants, leaving the more time-consuming finishing touches for the children. It might sound romantic but it wasn't. Jo remembered the hard work, with Ernest always driving them on. If Jo even straightened her back, she would have a lump of dirt thrown at her. All the way home Ernest told his children they were "*lazy snotty nosed whelps*". Jo considered this verbal abuse to be the most negative influence in her childhood. She attributed her sense of inferiority and emotional deprivation to this treatment.

The family picked hops in summer and potatoes in autumn. Tommy and Arthur shared a bucket, Jean and Jo another, Bet and Ernest a third. The boys disliked the fact that they were invariably beaten by the girls at potato picking. To keep up with the girls, the boys would cheat by putting lumps of earth into their sack. Of course, the farmer noticed straightaway and came out to complain. It was piecework. The farmer paid them sixpence a sack. Ernest earned well at certain times of year. A good week brought in £5 but some weeks he could earn as much as £30 when potato picking.

He needed it with ten children to feed. Ernest was not a heavy drinker. But he went to the pub at the weekend. He was an expert dart player and he could often win pints from his dart playing. Bet and Ernest were addicted to fags as they called them. Smoking was one of their few pleasures. Bet could never make ends meet so Ernest looked after the money. After buying the groceries, Ernest locked them in the sideboard. He never knew that Bet had found out how to take out the drawer above and reach down to get the vegetables. These she sold to the neighbours to get money for fags.

When they were not working, the King children attended Hartley Whitney School. School meals only cost a shilling a week, which most families could afford in those days. The Kings were the only family who could not pay and everyone knew it. The children resented being despised by teachers and pupils for being dirty and poor. To impress the other children and get attention, Jo used to show off by eating stinging nettles and claiming that they did not sting her. For Arthur, the PE (physical education) classes were the most embarrassing because they had to remove their shoes. When the Kings got a new pair of socks, they wore them until they dropped off their feet. Their socks stank and they were full of holes.

The King children were often absent and the truancy officer was a frequent caller at their hut. When Arthur joined the school aged ten, he was put in the C stream. By the time, he left at fifteen he had graduated to the A stream despite all the missed schooling. The Kings might have been the dregs of society but they were bright. Only Tommy never learned to read or write. Jo's education came from books. She was convinced that she had learned little apart from what she had read in the school library. Jo and Tommy were close, having spent the time in the orphanage together. It was Arthur who stood apart from the beginning. Arthur was the oldest and the first to leave. He had an instinct for getting on in the world.

When Arthur left school, he worked for eighteen months in the Huntley and Palmer biscuit factory at Reading. Up until 1958, two years National Service was compulsory for all young men once they reached eighteen. Arthur knew that he did not want to go into the army. He was shorter than average and he thought that he would be picked on by the tough army types. He had decided that the Royal Air Force might be a more educated and refined institution. To gain the advantage he went along in 1953 and volunteered when he was still seventeen. He could have signed on for three years in the RAF but he wanted to be a mechanic so he agreed to four years.

Arthur was careful with his money from the start. While working in the factory, he made loan repayments on a push bike. When he was eighteen, he wrote home excitedly with his plans to use his savings to buy a greenhouse for a market gardening business when he got out of the RAF. Bet wrote back to say that Ernest desperately needed £50 to buy a motor bike so he could get work further afield. Trustingly Arthur sent the £50 by return of post. Needless to say, he never heard about getting his money back. After the initial four years in the RAF Arthur spent a year back in the world outside. But finding that he could not get on, he went back to the RAF. He spent nine years in all as an airframe fitter, tightening bolts on the hydraulics and pneumatics for planes. Arthur admitted that he had never been practical and was never cut out to be a good mechanic.

In 1959 Arthur married Doreen Ellingworth. Trevor loaned them his vintage Rolls Royce for the wedding. Mr Ellingworth had his own business, a successful jewellery shop in Egham, and Doreen was privately educated. Doreen had turned Arthur down initially. She was not looking for a husband. But Arthur persisted and finally she accepted him. After their marriage, they lived on the RAF base at Abingdon, Oxfordshire. The RAF allowed their staff to spend one day a week in education. Arthur, resolving to make the most of the opportunity, enrolled in a course at technical college. He studied for a building ONC and they bought a small piece of land.

While the house was being built, they lived in a caravan on the site with their two young children. David was born in October 1962 and Louise in March 1964. In winter, Doreen had to negotiate the field with a pram just to do her daily groceries shopping. She put on wellington boots and then changed into proper shoes to walk into the town. Doreen told me how disciplined they were with their budget in order to save money. Each week became a competition to see if they could live more cheaply than the previous week. They had a tiny budget for groceries and lived on soup during the week.

While in the RAF, a friend of Arthur's suggested the idea of going into the fish and chip trade. When he was thirty, Arthur decided to buy his first shop in partnership with his father-in-law. Many people assumed that Arthur benefited from his father-in-law's capital. However, Arthur insisted on being an equal partner from the start. Over the next thirty years, he managed his own shops as well as entering into partnerships with his shop managers. Eventually he set up a limited company with a head office and computerised accounts. By the time we were teenagers, Jo used to refer to him as a millionaire but they were never extravagant with their money.

# Jo leaves the Nissen hut and later marries Trevor

At fifteen it was expected that Jo would make her own way in the world. She had nowhere to live so she worked as a nanny. Jo explained: *"I left the hut three months from my fifteenth birthday in 1953 because Bet left with the three smallest babies and told my father that she would not come back until I left. This I was told about a year later by her eldest daughter Jean. It seems that Bet thought this would get Jean back home as she had left the year before and gave the excuse that it was because of me. I am very grateful to them now as I think it was one of the best things that happened to me although I did not think so at the time. I was to spend the next three years in and out of lodgings sometimes having to sleep outside. All the time with a very big chip on my shoulder.*

*I was a pain to everyone who tried to help me. From fifteen to eighteen I spent running away from the past by hiding away in the cinema. It was my escape from life and people. I would do anything to go to the cinema. On my day off I would go three times and on my birthday. If I ran out of films in Basingstoke I would go to Reading and Odiham. Whether I could get back or not did not bother me. I just found a barn and slept in it for the night and arrived home the next day not expecting my employer to mind. I was in the end returned to my father because I was such a pain to my employer who was at the time the manager of the Red Lion Hotel in Basingstoke and I was nanny to their little boy Jeremy. They stood so much and then sent me home to my father."*

Ernest did not hesitate to kick out difficult offspring but they all went back later including Jo. She admitted herself that she was a troublesome teenager. When Jo was evicted from the hut, she resented what she saw as her father's rejection of her. After her marriage, Jo refused to ever see her father again. She could not accept losing the battle for his affections to the woman in his life.

*"Within three months of returning home I was smoking, drinking and going out with men none of which I had done until then. Because I spent most of my time on my own, I had not learned anything about sex. At eighteen, I did not know that if you had sex you might have a baby. After all, I had been sexually abused off and*

on since I was about four years of age and nothing had happened to teach me this. In fact, at eighteen I did not connect the abuse that I received with what happened in marriage.

*I had avoided men up to this point in my life. I would have continued to avoid them if they had not come after me. I was to be raped by a soldier from Aldershot Barracks. And not having anyone to tell at home I told the foreman at work because I liked him a lot. This started an affair between us. His name was Larry. He was married and had twin boys. He must have had an operation to stop him giving me a baby because it lasted some six months. He did not talk to me about the possibility of getting pregnant or I would not have been ignorant of such things. His wife caught us together one day and slapped my face and that ended the affair."*

Sometimes it was difficult to know how to interpret some of Jo's stories. She was fond of the word abuse. She probably used the word rape more readily than most of us would. She may have felt she had no control over events or just that she later regretted what had happened. Within ignorant communities, there is little sense of right and wrong. The stronger ones (older males) take what they can get and the vulnerable ones (children) are too ignorant or too frightened to complain. If a man or older boy takes advantage of girls, relatives or not, there's often little that the girls can do about it. Arthur had little sympathy for Jo's claimed ignorance, commenting that even young children knew the basic facts of life in the country because of the proximity to the animals and farming.

Jo recounted stories from her youth without shame but she omitted explicit details of the sexual aspects of her life. She justified her promiscuity in terms of a woman's instinctive drive to have a family. She tended to romanticise her relationships with men, even if they were fleeting affairs. When she was eighteen Jo became pregnant. *"I met a sailor called Brian Ashton when I went on holiday to Lea-on-Solent and fell in love on the rebound of my affair with Larry. When my boyfriend told me I might be having a baby, I was stunned. I did not believe him. He told me to go and see my doctor, who informed me that I was indeed pregnant. My doctor was so taken by my ignorance that he found a mother and baby home which took in fourteen- and fifteen-year olds."*

The home was a mental hospital but Jo attributed her condition to ignorance: both a lack of education in her own upbringing and being surrounded by uninformed attitudes. Jo learned the hard way but she never seemed to learn. She refused to have anything to do with the father of the baby because she believed that he had made her pregnant without her consent. Even after all her experiences, my mother could still be amazingly unworldly. It was perhaps this childlike naivety about life that caused the doctors to conclude that she lacked social maturity. When her baby girl was born, Jo would not agree to have her adopted but she also could not take her home. So her baby, Stephanie, was sent to a nursery in Winchester.

Soon after this Jo and Trevor met in a cafe in Camberley, Surrey. A former boyfriend of Jo's, called Sonny, had introduced them. From the beginning the personal chemistry worked well. Trevor proposed after a few weeks but Jo turned him down because she wanted to keep Stephanie. Trevor explained that his family would not accept an illegitimate child. A friend advised Jo to marry Trevor and have Stephanie adopted. Slowly Jo accepted that she was never going to be able to have the baby, so reluctantly she agreed to have the baby adopted and married Trevor. She had seen Stephanie only once since she was born because the nursery was so far away.

My parents married in July 1958 in Lightwater, Surrey after knowing each other just a few months. Trevor was thirty-eight and Jo was twenty. Jo's father and stepmother were not told about the wedding. Trevor was worried they might turn up and embarrass his parents who drove all the way from Durham in their Rolls Royce. It was an unlikely match. Jo had always been shy. Now she was overwhelmed by the Hare's money and class. Dr and Mrs Hare were shocked by Jo's commonness but she was young and pretty. What more could they wish for in a daughter-in-law? At my father's age, his parents must have been despairing of his marrying at all.

At six feet three and a half inches tall, Trevor was over a foot taller than his bride. He was as handsome and charming as the film stars Jo idolised. They honeymooned on the island of Ischia, in the bay of Naples. Jo had never been abroad before and, with her well-spoken husband by her side, she must have felt that all her dreams had come true. Trevor, on the other hand, found his new wife a trial. She moaned about the heat. He left her at the hotel while he made his own forays into the Italian nightlife. During the early years of their marriage Trevor undertook the social education of his wife, correcting her grammar and pronunciation. He taught her to cook. The West End musical 'My Fair Lady' was a hit in London at the time and no doubt lent some glamour to their marriage. Given that Jo had grown up in a hut, it was amazing that she adapted at all.

Around this time, Trevor inherited some capital from a relative and bought a large gabled house near Lightwater in Surrey. He named it Howlish after his grandparents' house in the North of England. Until now he had lived in London flats paid for by his parents. So, this was the first property that he owned outright. The novelty of having a family home kept him busy initially. For a few months, he had fun working on the garden, which had a stream running through it. The original plan was that he would commute daily up to London from Bagshot to his job in Victoria. But from Camberley it took an hour to reach London Waterloo. So later Trevor began staying up in London during the week. At weekends when he came to Lightwater, he always brought a friend with him.

Trevor didn't see any reason why his marriage should change anything. So he continued with his life much as before. Trevor had a natural authority because he was significantly older, because he was more educated and because of his inherited money. He continued to travel abroad without his wife. Trevor could travel cheaply because he worked as ground staff for BOAC. He was entitled to discounted airfares on long-haul flights. Trevor was good looking, well-spoken and charming. With money to spend and a gregarious nature, he made friends easily. This helped keep his holidays cheap because he stayed with people he met on his travels.

After the birth of their first child, Anne, in May 1959 life continued much the same as before except that Trevor now stayed in London for longer periods. I was born two years later in March 1961. My feet were turned in. They had to be bandaged tightly together until I was six months old to correct them. Jo found the weekly hospital visits upsetting because I screamed when the bandages were put back on again. Trevor stayed mainly in London after that, where and with whom Jo never knew. When he did come home, she had to make sure that we were in bed because he expected his evenings to be quiet. Jo became increasingly isolated. She made friends with Jenny, another young mother. Jenny's husband baby-sat sometimes during the week so that the two women could go out together.

## Trevor often absented himself from the marriage

Soon after I was born, Trevor set off for San Francisco on a holiday. He was there about a week when he called to tell Jo that he had been involved in a serious accident while riding pillion on a motor bike. He had been taken to hospital but he had no travel insurance. He needed Jo to come and sort things out for him. First Jo had to get a visa for herself and two babies. My older sister Anne was still in nappies. Then she had to persuade BOAC to allow the usual staff discounted fare of £38 return. They did not think a broken ankle justified a transatlantic trip, but Jo was concerned. Trevor could spend hundreds in a day with no means of repaying it.

Jo called the Hares to ask them whether they could help. Mrs Hare thought that Jo should go but said that they were too old to help with the children. By this time, Anne was two but she was still not walking. I was just six weeks old and Jo was breastfeeding. In those days, it was not possible to breastfeed on board an aircraft. The doctor advised Jo to stop her breasts producing milk by winding bandages tightly around her chest. After this I was bottle-fed. As soon as the plane landed, we were taken straight to the hospital. We stayed with Trevor's friends. Mayben, the wife of the motorcycle driver, found someone to help with the money to pay the hospital bill. Her sixteen-year-old daughter was fond of looking after babies so Jo managed to fit in a day or two of sightseeing in San Francisco. Trevor was left with an ugly scar on his ankle and a conviction that we should never have a boyfriend with a motorcycle.

As a baby, Anne had rolls of fat around her body like a small Michelin man. As a toddler she could move whole pieces of furniture single-handed. Jo was concerned but since her own doctor and her father-in-law, also a doctor, never said anything Jo thought perhaps she was just being overly anxious. Anne caught a cold and being so far from home Jo took her to a doctor. The doctor showed little interest in the cold but asked detailed questions about Anne's development. Jo was relieved because it had been bothering her for some time that something might be wrong with Anne. The doctor advised her to consult the children's hospital in Great Ormond Street, London. On their return to London, my parents took Anne to Great Ormond Street. The consultant diagnosed Anne as having Hunter-Hurler Syndrome, a chemical or metabolic condition. Her case was not particularly severe but there was no cure available.

Anne was mentally handicapped. Her disability was evidenced mainly through her difficulty with speech. Anne's face was noticeably round and flat (called mongoloid). Sometimes when she was talking, she would half-close her eyes and roll them upwards. Later, during my first pregnancy in 1990, I called Great Ormond Street to ask about the risk of passing on Anne's condition. Based on seeing a recent photograph of Anne, Dr Baraitser wrote: *"Clearly your sister has neither Hurler nor Hunter syndrome but looking at her fingers and general form she does, in all likelihood, have one of the other mucopolysacharidoses, i.e. Scheie syndrome."* He described Anne's condition as a very rare disorder.

Jo's younger brother Tommy married Frances Cooper and they had a daughter, Helen, a year after I was born. Anne and Helen used to play together until her mother started to worry that Anne's condition might affect Helen's development. Later Frances became jealous of the close relationship between Tommy and his sister Jo. She stopped Tommy from seeing Jo for over ten years. It was about this time that Trevor asked Tommy's mother-in-law, Mrs Cooper, to have Anne because Jo was having difficulty coping with her.

Trevor was embarrassed by Anne and her condition. So, he was relieved to have her taken off their hands. Mrs Cooper knew Anne through the family connection and was willing to give Anne a home. At first Mrs Cooper had her for short stays but soon Anne went to live with her permanently. While Anne was living with Mrs Cooper, she attended a day school in Bracknell for mentally handicapped children. Here she became a favourite of one of the teachers, Mrs Peters. One Christmas when Anne was four years old, neither Mrs Cooper nor her parents could have Anne over the holidays. When Mrs Peters heard, she invited Anne to join her family's Christmas.

A few years later when Mrs Cooper told Trevor that she could not have Anne, he found a boarding school for backward children in Broadstairs, Kent. Anne stayed there until she was eleven and she spent the school holidays with Mrs Peters. When the time came for Anne to move up to the senior school, they said that she was not up to the required standard. Trevor was relieved when Mrs Peters solved his problem by volunteering to have Anne live with her. Anne must have been overjoyed to be living permanently with Mrs Peters in Crowthorne, Berkshire, which by then was her home.

Initially doctors told my parents that Anne wouldn't live beyond her teens. Later though the opinion was that Anne had the same life expectancy as anyone else. Jo always insisted that she wanted custody of Anne even when I could see that having permanent care of Anne would be difficult because she needed full-time care. Anne thrived on the one-to-one attention she got from Mrs Peters. Caring for Anne was like caring for a small child. Mrs Peters accompanied Anne on her occasional trips to London to visit Trevor for lunch because he would not have known how to deal with her by himself. In later years, Trevor suggested that Anne's condition was not serious and that in many ways she was like his sister Barbara. This comment made me realise how little he understood. Barbara sometimes used a behaviour of childlike innocence as a form of protection against the world. She didn't like to take responsibility in awkward situations but she had full command of all her faculties.

Soon after my first birthday Trevor decided to sell Howlish and move back to London. He bought a mews house in Bayswater, which he made into two flats. He let out the top flat and we lived in the other. For a few months, my parents employed a Belgian au pair. Michelle was an adventurous young woman. Jo enjoyed her companionship and together they explored gay bars and some of the seedier London venues. The two young women shared a liking for potentially dangerous situations and a total disregard for social propriety. Finally, Michelle came back one night high on drugs and Trevor escorted her to the train station. Jo and Michelle stayed in touch for years, visiting each other on more than one occasion.

Years later, Arthur's wife Doreen told me how shocked she was by Jo's stories of her sexual escapades whilst living in London.

Apparently on one occasion Jo went home with a man she had just met on the top of a double-decker bus. Jo liked to talk about her adventures. She enjoyed the attention she got and it never bothered her what people might think. Jo had little need to make stories up. The truth was probably shocking enough for most people. My serious nature would never allow me to live as my parents lived. But I appreciated that they were always themselves without the usual pretence. Most adults are much too concerned about being judged by others. Equally, many adults live very mundane lives.

My sister Sarah was born in February 1963, a month early. It was a traumatic birth assisted by vacuum extraction, a degrading and painful procedure. The procedure was relatively rare. There were students and many other observers who came to watch. Years later, I also experienced giving birth in a hospital. There is little privacy. A woman's most intimate anatomy goes on public display. Anyone who is invited into the room can gaze at your genitals without so much as an acknowledgement. A woman ceases to exist as a person and becomes a conduit for the baby to appear through. Afterwards, Jo suffered severe depression and she was put on medication.

A year later, Jo decided that the marriage was contributing to her problems. In July 1964, she asked to take a break with Mary, a friend of Trevor's who lived near their old house in Lightwater. Mary was rich and eccentric. She could be embarrassingly loud in public but she was good company. After the two weeks ended, Jo could not face returning to London. Mary agreed Jo could stay on. Jo wrote: *"Trevor came to see me once and I know if he had said that he needed me in any way I would have gone back to him. I thought I was in love with him still but I realise now it was profound pity. But it was obvious that he could not see what the problem was. He had done nothing wrong in his way of thinking."*

When Jo left Trevor, she wrote to Dr and Mrs Hare to ask them if they would help her. She said she could not go on the way things were. The Hares advised her to hold on to the nice home Trevor had provided her with. Granny offered to support her daughter-in-law if she stayed in Bayswater. But Jo was determined to leave and file for divorce. Trevor blamed Jo's friend Jenny who he believed had given Jo the idea that she would get a share of his money. In fact, Trevor owned relatively little in his own name. Jo had almost no money while staying with Mary. In summer, she cut the toes out of our shoes to get more wear out of them. Then one day Jo went out and left her children with Mary. She returned to find Mary helping us to paint the walls with nail varnish. Mary was heading for a mental breakdown and Jo realised she would have to leave.

*"I rented a flat in Fleet, Hampshire, near Jenny but the rent was as much as what I was receiving from Trevor £8 a week. Trevor gave this amount to me freely. I got a job stacking shelves but by the time I paid the rent and Jenny to look after the girls I did not have much left. I had no knowledge of council housing or social security and no one to advise me. I rang my in-laws and asked them to have Jane and Sarah while I went to London to find a home for us. They had not seen the children since before I left Trevor in 1964. Trevor had only seen them once when he came to see me at Mary's two years before. I was not successful in London in finding a home for us. Dr and Mrs Hare sent the children to Trevor who was now in Battersea and letting the house in Bayswater. I moved to Battersea to be near them. I tried the council there but they would not house me."*

In 1966 the divorce was finally granted. Initially, custody was awarded to Jo. However, following her action of leaving us with him, Trevor applied to the high court for custody. The night Jo heard that Trevor had won custody, she went to a pub in Battersea and got drunk. She planned to take an overdose of pills but a man who lived in the same building stayed with her until she was sober. Jo decided to go to Guernsey for the summer with the man who had saved her life. He turned out to be an alcoholic and Jo was naive enough to trust him with looking after her money. He spent it all on booze and they had to do an early morning flight from the hotel. The authorities threatened to send her back to England. But Jo got a job doing laundry. She agreed to stay for three months until the money was repaid and the hotelier agreed to drop the charges.

## The Hares use their money to end the custody battle

Jo should have had a strong case for custody. The courts usually awarded custody to the mother and Trevor had no interest in raising children. But there had been stays in mental hospital as well as the difficulty Jo had coping with small children. After she left Trevor, Jo had asked him to have the children while she went to Brussels to visit Michelle, her former au pair. She was judged to be an unreliable parent and perhaps lacking in the dedication society expects of a mother towards her children. Jo concluded that the legal system was biased against her because of Trevor's education and his family's money. The fact was that in the 1960s, the UK divorce laws were drafted heavily in the man's favour. There was little sympathy for a woman walking out on a marriage and a home.

In those days, a woman was expected to accept marriage as a means of raising children no matter how badly a man behaved. Jo's view was that Trevor's misdemeanours, listed in her divorce petition, proved that his unreasonable behaviour had deprived her of a home. When Trevor bought the house in Battersea, he had not yet sold the house in Bayswater. Since he had two homes and she had none, she expected a court to agree that he should give one of them to her. Jo did not understand the difference between what she deemed to be justice and what the law allowed. Her legal-aid solicitor said that she was unlikely to get anything. He advised her that she would have to prove that her children were in danger.

On one of our visits to Gidea Park, Jo took us to an interview with the social services. They wanted to know if we liked living with Trevor. The truth was that we didn't live with him. We lived with a nanny. Their questions seemed critical of Trevor and I remember feeling under pressure to defend him. I did not blame Trevor for the deficiencies in our care. For a start, I didn't know any better but I was also unaware of his parental responsibilities. Frankly, asking a child to judge its parents according to adult values is pointless. I loved my parents. They gave me more attention than other adults.

One time when Jo collected us from Daphne's, she had to wash Sarah's coat because it was so filthy. Both of us had fleas. She reported Trevor to the NSPCC and they arranged to inspect the London flat. That morning Daphne overslept and we did not dare wake her. When she finally woke up, she was furious with us. Nothing changed after this visit. At the next hearing, Jo brought an action against Trevor for neglect. When the case came up, the court was told that Daphne was ill and could not attend. Trevor made light of the headlice, saying that everyone caught lice at some time or other. All these court hearings were costing the Hares a fortune.

So our grandparents decided to pay for Sarah and me to board at private school. They had previously offered to pay school fees for their other grandchildren, John and Sue, our Aunt Barbara's children. But her husband Alastair politely declined the offer as perhaps many people would as an initial response. It was subsequently difficult for him to complain when Granny paid for our education. Alastair was reminded that he had turned down the offer. He, in turn, made the point later to his wife that a sincere offer to contribute would not have been made just one time. The Hares justified holding onto their money as the old-fashioned virtue of thrift but it sometimes came across as the meanness of the rich.

When Trevor broke the news to Daphne, she was not pleased. It meant that she had to find another job and somewhere to live. She confronted me over the move as if it was my fault in some way. Some months later, during a school holiday, Trevor took us to see Daphne. She was living with Patrick and Christopher in a high-rise block of council flats in Wandsworth. We had never been fond of her. But seeing the circumstances in which she was living gave me a glimpse of what my life might have been like if Granny had not paid for us to go away to school. It all seemed like another world. The social disadvantage was apparent to me because of the neglect, including lower standards of cleanliness and less adult attention.

Once Jo had the council flat in Gidea Park, she came close to getting custody. Trevor's action of sending us to boarding school far from London, had given her the justification for another hearing. Trevor's legal team, paid for by Dr and Mrs Hare, used the fact that Jo had already given up a baby before she met Trevor to weaken her claim. But the judge was cross with Trevor for changing the children's situation without the court's permission. For a while Jo thought that she would win us back. The court broke for lunch to allow Dr and Mrs Hare to decide whether they would still pay for our education if Jo was given custody. The answer was: no, they would not. The court decided that it was in our interests to be privately educated, which left Trevor as our legal guardian.

The hearings were not only expensive but also embarrassing for the Hares. The domestic and personal details of their son's life were publicly aired and documented in a court of law. Jo believed that the Hares had acted out of spite because she had left Trevor. I certainly never felt that our grandparents were especially fond of us. We had no expectations as children. But looking back, there were no presents, holidays or even hugs that you might expect from grandparents. They were rich but not generous people. At the Sneep, the full boarders had a period of supervision on Saturday morning to write letters home. Sarah and I wrote each week to Jo, Trevor and Granny. At senior school, I phoned my parents every week from the coin phone box. I continued to write regularly to Granny as a teenager. This written correspondence probably represented my closest relationship with my grandmother. She revealed more interest in my affairs than she ever had face-to-face.

When Sarah left Queen Anne's she wrote to Granny to thank her for paying the fees for her boarding school education. Trevor dropped some strong hints that it would be a good idea if I followed suit but I never did. There were a number of reasons why I did not want to thank Granny for my schooling. Firstly, Jo had always said that she only paid the fees to keep us away from her. Trevor never referred to past events so I had only Jo's explanation of events. But since he never looked after us himself, it was difficult to understand any positive explanations for why Trevor wanted custody of us.

There was no doubt in my mind that I had benefited from a private education. However, the cost to my personal happiness had been high and I could not easily feel grateful. I also questioned Granny's motivation in paying our school fees because of the personality conflict between us. She was used to being obeyed. I disliked the influence Granny had over my father even in his fifties. One time, Trevor asked a friend to cut his hair before we drove up North. When I asked him why he needed to do this, he said that he was sick of Granny's comments. Apparently, she objected to men with hair below the collar. I was amazed that her opinion bothered him.

When we were children, Granny had always asked the hairdresser to cut our hair very short (a boy's hairstyle). Towards the end of our time at the Sneep, Granny could no longer walk. She asked

Frances, her home-help, to take us. For the first time, the hairdresser asked me how I would like to have my hair cut. I said truthfully that I wanted to grow my hair. When I returned to the bungalow, I anticipated Granny's displeasure. I had asserted my own choice in direct contradiction to her own unspoken wishes. I was aware of the awkward silence but she made no comment.

The next time, Granny had evidently given some thought to how she might coerce me into conforming. I wrote in my diary *"This morning I was extremely vexed. I felt myself practically fuming inside. Granny called me into the kitchen. She asked me if I would have my hair trimmed. No, I have had it done already. Then she said that we were always stubborn after we had been to stay with Mum."* Sarah agreed to have her hair cut *"just to please Granny"*.

Granny told me to accompany Sarah to the hairdresser. It was obviously some form of punishment. I got no support from Trevor who told Sarah that he did not know what had come over me. I could never understand why anyone would let themselves be bullied. As usual Trevor never discussed the topic with me. I always felt that Granny was always putting others down, especially her own children. Once in their fifties, Trevor and Barbara talked about taking a boat trip across the North Sea just for fun. Granny quickly quashed the idea as ridiculous and they didn't go. To be fair, they were both inclined to spend money on useless but expensive things. No doubt Granny knew that she was often expected to pay the bill.

I felt that my grandmother lacked a sense of humour or the ability to know when you need to let people make their own mistakes. The gap in our ages certainly meant that she never talked to me as an equal. This was unknown to her generation. Barbara was more accepting of this Edwardian style of parental control than Trevor. Once the young Barbara, who had the looks of a Hollywood film star, confided in her mother her nervousness before a party. Presumably to discourage any vanity, Granny responded *"What colossal conceit to think that anyone will be looking at you!"* Maybe she intended to help but her tone could be very severe. I believe that this kind of criticism, with no praise, leads to adults who lack confidence in themselves. Although I often felt my parents were not interested in my life, I am so grateful they never criticised.

# Holidays with Jo in the only home we ever knew

After six years of legal proceedings Jo was offered a divorce settlement of around £4,000, which she used to buy herself a house. Her friend, Jenny, was now living in Kingsclere. Jo decided to settle in this pleasant Hampshire village where she had a friend nearby. She bought a semi-detached house on the same housing estate as Jenny. Now that she had a home of her own, Jo asked a solicitor what her chances were of winning back custody. He said there was no chance. Nothing had changed since Trevor had gained custody.

After buying the house, Jo had enough money for fitted carpets, some furniture and a Hoover. The rest she acquired as she went along. Most of it was bought second-hand from advertisements in shop windows. Finally, Jo had a home of her own and with our future committed to boarding school, she decided to get on with her life. She got a ginger cat, calling him Asher after the actress. A couple of years later, she named a second cat Seymour, after the other Jane. When Jo found herself missing her daughters too much, she invited other children to go walking with her and Simon. The house had two double bedrooms, a box room and an upstairs bathroom. The house had gas for cooking but no central heating, which was still considered an optional extra at the start of the 1970s.

In winter, the house got cold at night and we went to bed with hot water bottles. I remember placing mine in the top part of the bed while I brushed my teeth. Then I would curl up just under the cover and slowly work the hot water bottle down the bed with my feet until I could stretch my legs out all the way to the bottom. When it got really cold, we went to bed wearing socks and jumpers. In the mornings, we woke to single-paned windows frozen both inside and out. Jo went down early to light the coal fire in the living room. We only ventured down once we could huddle in front of the fire with one side of us roasting and the other still freezing. Later she invested in a small paraffin heater, which sat in the hallway at the bottom of the stairs and took the edge off the iciness of the upstairs.

Jo worked hard to provide a loving home. The house at Kingsclere was the only real home Sarah and I ever knew. Our holidays in Kingsclere were free of rules and routine. In the morning, we watched children's programmes like Thunderbirds and Hammy Hamster with Simon. We helped ourselves to breakfast cereal, which we ate in front of the telly. I liked to spend time helping Jo. Every day, we went down to the village together to shop for food. Jo received social security benefits for herself and Simon. Any extra money she received for us during holidays was spent on food. Jo's budget was always limited and we could only buy as much as we could carry. We did the round of the shops: bread, sugar and tins from the grocery store, fruit and vegetables from the green grocers and meat from the butcher. The house was at the top of a hill so we had to carry the groceries in bags all the way back up the hill.

I was an affectionate child. When I was small, I enjoyed cuddling up with each of my parents. Jo was a good parent both in terms of demonstrating affection and because she had an even temper. When we were small, we would take turns to sit in the armchair with Jo, either by her side or on her lap being cuddled. We were always her babies. She told us affectionately that we were beautiful. Jo had a vernacular all of her own: food was grub, dessert was pud, vegetables were veg and so on. She kept a chip pan on the gas hob. The food was always simple but tasty. A popular meal was fried eggs with baked beans and chip potatoes. She also made shepherd's pie, spaghetti bolognaise and chicken casserole. We had simple desserts such as tinned steamed puddings and banana custard.

Jo loved her garden and her houseplants, which filled every windowsill both upstairs and downstairs. I enjoyed walking around the garden listening to her plans for her garden. A public footpath ran along the back of the house. There was a large hole up by the back hedge. Simon and his friends spent many happy hours digging and playing in this hole. Simon also had a paddling pool, which we used in summer to cool down. Each year Jo built up her tan slowly whenever there was a sunny day. She was pleased that by early summer many people assumed that she must have been abroad.

We went walking through the fields and woods both in summer and in winter. During these walks, Jo would reminisce about her childhood and tell us of her adventures in the countryside where she grew up. In the summer months, we played outdoors for hours. There was a playing field further up the hill with a set of swings.

Sarah and I were nervous of meeting the local children, especially the boys, in case they decided to pick on us for being different. We used to venture into the countryside by ourselves. We played endless camps and adventure games. In the late summer, we played in the haystacks until the farmers, or the jockeys from the nearby horse racing stables, caught us and told us to play somewhere else.

On rainy days, we played Scrabble or Bingo and did jigsaw puzzles together. Jo was often knitting. It was cheaper to knit jumpers than buy them in the shops. While she knitted jumpers for us, Sarah and I knitted for our teddies. We played cards or watched telly, which was rarely switched off in winter. The television was black and white. Some of the knobs had fallen off or did not work anymore. Eventually the rental company stopped coming to collect the rent. Jo and I often watched an old film together. Jo enjoyed the movies from the 1950s and '60s with the glamorous stars. She had a couple of tattered books kept from her youth with photographs and the life stories of the film stars. I enjoyed romantic musicals such as The Student Prince (1954) and Camelot (1967).

Initially Jo had a small radio but it broke and was never replaced. She also had an old record player and a collection of second-hand singles. Some evenings, we danced to classic pop songs from the fifties and sixties such as Jailhouse Rock or Michelle. My parents both liked listening to songs and their tastes were not especially sophisticated. They liked a good tune. I was similar. I have never been especially interested in music but I have always enjoyed songs. I enjoyed Andrew Lloyd Webber's musicals with Tim Rice's thought-inspiring lyrics. Much later, I appreciated Queen for the poignant lyrics and the vocal range of Freddie Mercury's voice.

Jo eventually won the use of one of the public vegetable allotments in the village despite considerable scepticism from the male community. She worked it for many years, earning respect from the men. She dug her allotment every year by hand with a fork and spade whereas most of the men, having more money at their disposal, had rotavators. She explained to me that her method was better because she could remove the couch grass, which the rotavators just ploughed back into the ground. Sometimes I went to keep her company and I helped with bean harvesting or weeding.

Jo did most of her own house decoration inside and out. One day when she was moving a heavy ladder to paint one of the upstairs windows, she damaged her back. It was to be a problem for years. Then one time in Tunisia, some ill-advised windsurfing solved the problem. It evidently doesn't always pay to do the sensible thing! Jo was proud that she could wire up a household plug. She would comment that married women were useless at practical chores because they had a man around to do everything for them. Yet we had a sideboard for years with broken hinges. We had to lift the door off and balance it back on each time we used the cupboard.

Jo joined the village public library. She was a great reader and especially enjoyed biographies. Once Simon started school, Jo had more free time. She took on a part-time job cleaning and washing-up in a small restaurant in the village. She also had a job cleaning a large house in the village. She could only work part-time hours otherwise she would lose her benefits. Later she worked at a local chicken farm packing eggs. Jo had no washing machine so she had to take her laundry down the hill to the launderette in the village.

Naturally I was conscious of the social differences between Jo's house and the houses of other families we visited. For example, Jo kept her butter in the packet either in the fridge or out on the kitchen top. In middle class homes, they always had a butter dish and there was a butter knife. Jams or marmalade were served with a separate spoon. Jo's butter and jam got mixed up with each other over time. I liked the simple approach. I decided that although I appreciated social sophistication, I didn't like pretentiousness.

Now that Jo had a family home, Arthur and Doreen came with their children and brought presents for us just before Christmas. I don't think we gave them anything back because there was no money. Jo resented their money but she also couldn't tolerate her brother's domineering and chauvinistic manner. One summer we went to stay for a week in relative style in a small hotel in Bournemouth. We spent our holiday sitting on the beach but it was very cold and windy. Sand was blown into the cucumber and spam sandwiches. We all read books and helped Jo with her endless books of crossword puzzles. My Uncle Arthur came with his car to take us home at the end so I assume that he must have paid for the holiday.

Sarah and I shared a room with bunk beds in Kingsclere. We were used to living out of a suitcase. Simon had the box room. As a single parent, Jo naturally looked after Simon's health, social development and progress at school. Our education was out of her hands. Sarah and I were more like visitors to her house rather than her full responsibility as Simon was. Trevor took us to the dentist after prompting from Mrs Herring. He never engaged though and used to wait in the car outside. In London we went by ourselves.

When Anne came to stay, she had to sleep in a bed in Jo's room. Anne irritated us because she kept moaning. Simon was always very good at including her if he was not playing with his friends. Sometimes one of the children would spot that Anne was backward and start making fun of her. It was difficult for us to protect her and if things got unpleasant, we would just go home. Anne's life with Mrs Peters, sheltered her from normal society. She was aware that she was different to us. This realisation seemed to frustrate her sometimes. So Anne often struggled in Kingsclere. As we were growing up, it became more difficult for her to spend time with us.

One summer when we were still pre-teens, Jo told me that Anne had been moving her hips rhythmically as she lay face down on a towel while we were sunbathing in the garden. Onlookers often assume that little girls are trying to satisfy some conscious erotic arousal as boys and men do. But they are much too young. Girls do not experience the same biological and physical arousal that boys do. I have concluded that little girls engage in an instinctive, rhythmic movement that has nothing to do with achieving orgasm. The activity provides comfort rather than being a result of arousal.

Years later I read Kinsey's comment that this instinctive thrusting movement mimics the male role in intercourse. When I discovered orgasm in my late teens, I used this same position instinctively while focusing on fantasy. I pushed my fingers down from the vulva and either side of the labia but the anatomy involved was not explicit. Later I read Shere Hite and realised that it was the internal clitoral organ. But the most vital ingredient was my mind's ability to respond to explicit eroticism. In normal circumstances (when not masturbating) I had no consciousness of any erotic arousal even with a lover. This fact is core to understanding women's sexuality.

# PART III: MY FATHER'S FAMILY

## My paternal grandfather's family: The Hares

Trevor had a portrait of his grandmother Hare (who he irreverently referred to as The Welsh Witch) hanging over the door of his room in Battersea. Goodness knows why he kept it because he made no secret of the fact that he had no fondness for family. He said, *"You may not be able to choose your family but, thank God, you can choose your friends!"* Trevor was not one to reminisce. He never talked about his childhood. I got an account of the family many years later from his cousin George, whose own childhood had been much less indulged than my father's. George Caldwell had many educated interests and he read much more widely than my father. He spent years researching his own family history and family tree.

Trevor's paternal grandmother, Mervanwey Williams was known as Missie. She had grown up in Betws-y-Coed, North Wales. When she married Sam Hare, they lived at Howlish Hall, a substantial house on the hill above Eldon Colliery, close to the market town of Bishop Auckland, County Durham. The colliery lay below the house and was a dismal, dirty place. Sam Hare was manager of the colliery. As long as he kept the price of coal below ten shillings a ton, he and his family had a rent-free house with servants, a car and a chauffeur. The family enjoyed a good standard of living up to and after the Great War of 1914. For a time, Sam was president of the Institute of Mining Engineers. They had a flat on the Edgware Road for when he attended functions in London. When he retired, Sam was presented with a canteen of solid silver cutlery. Sam Hare died in 1937 and Missie moved to Scarborough where she died in 1947.

Sam and Missie had three sons. Victor, the youngest, was the only one not to study medicine. He took up his father's trade and became a colliery manager in Kent. The middle son, Jack, was originally engaged to my grandmother Elsie Walton but he went to Cape Town in South Africa where he met a girl called Kitty. He wrote to my grandmother explaining that he somehow found himself to be engaged to two girls at the same time. Elsie was quick to release him by telegram: 'Consider yourself free'. Jack went on to be an ear, nose and throat specialist in Harley Street, London.

The eldest son was known as Frank. Francis Frederick Trevor Hare was born in January 1886. Sam Hare was not in favour of the new public schools (fee paying but headed by a board of governors rather than a private owner). Sam sent his sons to board first at Morpeth Grammar School in Northumberland and later at Newcastle Grammar School. In the 1890s, an education of any kind was a privilege but the grammar schools were not as socially elitist as the public schools. Frank never acquired the arrogance and the affected accent of the public schools. He grew up playing billiards with the miners in the working men's clubs at his father's collieries. Frank was always proud of his North Country heritage.

After school Frank studied medicine at the Royal Victoria Infirmary in Newcastle upon Tyne and in due course he qualified as a doctor. The First World War intervened and he served in Mesopotamia as a captain in the army. After his discharge, he returned home. Unlike his brother Jack, Frank had failed his fellowship exams for the Royal College of Surgeons. Rather than resit his exams, Frank decided to start work immediately as a general practitioner. He borrowed the £2,500 for his medical practice from his father, which he repaid as soon as he was able.

Frank had been engaged to the daughter of a very rich man called Bartholomew. One day his prospective father-in-law informed Frank that, on marrying his daughter, he would be expected to add Bartholomew to his surname. Frank did not like the implication that he would not be master of his own house and the engagement was broken off. This happened around the time that Elsie Walton released his brother Jack from their engagement. It was agreed in the Hare household that Frank should not waste any time in making an offer for Elsie's hand. My grandparents were married in August 1917 and Granny said later: *"I got the one I wanted!"*.

Having a father who was a mining engineer gave Frank an advantage at the hospital because many of the admissions were from miners' families. In addition to his practice and hospital work, Frank was also compensations doctor for local collieries. He was later appointed honorary senior surgeon to Durham County Hospital, a post he held for over 30 years. As a young man, Frank cut a dashing figure as he tore around Durham in his small green Riley. He may not have been overly tactful, but he was good-natured, and offered his views with a certain naiveté. Frank was proud of his home and family but eager to help those less fortunate. Both he and Elsie were interested in politics, so topical issues were debated avidly at home.

Frank and Elsie Hare lived in The Tower, a large stone-built house overlooking the historic city of Durham. I visited the house many years later, while researching my family history. It was being used as a hotel, which gives some indication of the size. The house stands on a steep slope, with gardens below cut out of the hill on two levels. Downstairs in the basement were Frank's surgery, waiting room and dispensary. Patients used to call at the house and sit in the waiting room. Often, they could hear Elsie playing the grand piano above and later on the young Barbara practising. The house was set back from the road just enough to allow space for a garage and two matching Rileys: a black one for Frank and a grey one for Elsie.

There were steps up to the double front door and then more steps up into the central reception hall. Here they removed the old floorboards and replaced them with a new sprung floor for dancing. The Hares gave black-tie dinner parties with dancing afterwards. At the far side of the hall was a wide central flight of stairs going up to a half-landing and a stained-glass window. Throughout the house the architectural style was church Gothic. The dining room had large high windows looking out over the lawn and across to the ancient Cathedral of Durham City. They added new playrooms in the attics: a billiard room and another room for table tennis. There was even a sewing room at the top of the tower over the front door.

Each time their cousins the Caldwells visited, it seemed there was something new: either new decoration or new furniture. The Caldwells got the cast-offs. The morning room was at the bottom of the tower, left of the front door. It was a smart room with a blue fitted carpet, modern wall-lights, large radio-gramophone and comfortable furniture. At one time the suite was leather, which the Caldwells later inherited. The morning room was the living room and business centre of the house. My grandmother kept the books.

The telephone rang often and Elsie dealt with the calls. Off-duty, Frank sat with legs apart in front of the roaring fire. He smoked one cigarette after another in a slim holder, which he used as a blowpipe. He aimed badly and the butts often missed the fire grate.

My grandmother had two maids. They were miners' daughters who lived in the house with the family under a strict curfew. Elsie used to train one girl as a housemaid to assist with the house cleaning and the other as a cook to help her in the kitchen. She was always careful to treat the servants with respect and would not ask them to do something she was not be prepared to do herself. So, when a patient vomited in the waiting room it was Elsie who cleaned up.

During the war years Frank decided that the ration of one egg per week would be insufficient for the family. So, he acquired a dozen chickens and it was Elsie who had to feed and clean them. After the war, young women no longer wanted to work as live-in maids. A local woman, Annie, had previously helped the household with their annual spring-cleaning. Now Mrs Hare took her on as a full-time, but live-out, domestic help in the house. Later her daughter Frances took over. They also had a man to help in the garden.

My grandparents both enjoyed playing golf and bridge. Holidays included playing golf in Scotland at Gleneagles, Turnberry and other well-known courses. Sometimes they took a caravan behind the Riley and went touring. There were occasional holidays abroad. They also spent time at Scarborough where Frank's mother had a house. There were trips to London too. They used to drive down to the fashionable seaside resorts on the south coast for summer holidays. In those days, the Great North Road (later the A1) was a single-carriage road with little traffic. My grandparents often stayed at the Cumberland Hotel in London to break their journey south.

Wherever they travelled, Frank was very particular about his food. He insisted that his beef should be cooked just as he enjoyed it at home. He believed that only invalids should be fed chicken or fish. If these were offered for dinner at the hotel in Eastbourne, he would set off alone to dine further along the front or even take the train to London. He was accustomed to getting his own way. Frank was a traditional man and his authority at home absolute. He was reputed to say: *"I may not always be right but I am never wrong!"*

## My paternal grandmother's family: The Waltons

My grandmother's family lived at Crook, another colliery town on the edge of a coalfield, with Weardale beyond. In those days, Crook was an up-and-coming town. The railway arrived in 1842 and took the superior coking coal to as far away as Barrow-in-Furness in Lancashire. Thomas Walton was born in May 1857. His father was a building contractor but when he died from drink, there was little money. The three bothers Robert, William and Thomas had about seventeen guineas between them. Thomas was the youngest and he used his knowledge of horses to make money, buying and selling them in the marketplace. Together the brothers kept the building business going. Later they opened a soap factory followed by a leather factory. There was a building boom that started in the eighteen eighties and continued right up until the start of the First War. All three brothers could lay bricks and saw wood.

Thomas married Mary Simpson and they had five children. Harry, the eldest, died in his early thirties on a hospital ship bound for India during the First World War, which nearly broke his father's heart. Eleanor, known as Nellie, was born in April 1887 and Fred in December 1890. Elsie, my grandmother, was born in January 1893. Another son, Thomas, did not survive. Mary was an excellent housekeeper. She had grown up in a family of four sons and four daughters. Having been raised on a farm, Mary was skilled at skinning rabbits, sausage-making and gutting birds. She had a head for figures and assisted her husband with his building estimates. Mary was one of those people who could add up three columns of Pounds, Shillings and Pence just by running her fingers down them.

The Waltons lived at The Willows on Commercial Street, Crook. It is still there, right beside the main road, a red brick house with a conservatory on the side. They lived well and there were tennis parties as well as musical evenings. Both Nellie and Elsie played the piano to concert standard. Dances and balls were held in various town and church halls. The Waltons were at the upper end of local society and they had the first motorcars. They did not have a Lord

Mayor in those days but Thomas Walton was really No. 1 in Crook and head of the local Council. Every Sunday wearing his silk top hat and morning coat, he would march down to the church for Evensong. The younger members of the family had to sit in the family pew in the mornings. He travelled around town in a horse and carriage, wearing his top hat. He was a big man, six foot tall and straight backed. A non-smoker and a non-drinker, he enjoyed his food. There was a kindly twinkle in his eye but he had authority.

In 1914 Fred Walton went off to war. He was quickly promoted and ended up a colonel. He later became Deputy Lieutenant of the County, Grand Mason next to Lord Barnard. After the Great War the Colonel, as he was called, asked his father to retire and give him the firm. Thomas Walton removed his capital and told Fred that what was left 'was all his'. Fred had the woodworking shop with machinery and the steam engine to run it. He had horses, wagons and some motor wagons but no capital. Thomas continued to be a respected local figure. At the time of the Great Depression in 1926, the townsfolk marched up to the house and down the long drive to ask Thomas to find work for them. There were hordes of desperate people crowding right up to the glass of the front windows. They covered the lawn as far as one could see while Thomas addressed them from the front steps of the house. But there was no work.

Thomas Walton became partners with Sam Hare in a drift mine called Brusselton Colliery until the nationalisation of the coal mines. Later Thomas also invested in shipping. By 1939 he had five shipping lines (including the Walton, Dawson, Jubilee and Edwardian Lines). Each line had three or four ships sailing around the world. These were sold off as scrap to the Japanese just before World War II. The seaworthy ones continued until they were sunk by German U-boats in the Atlantic. Thomas Walton died in 1948.

The two girls, Nellie and Elsie, were sent to a boarding school run by a strict German headmistress at Saltburn on the Yorkshire coast. They detested both the school and the headmistress, who was remembered long afterwards for an unsightly fang that protruded over her lower lip. This school may have contributed to both sisters having a stern and authoritarian approach as mothers. The society and the time in which they grew up in was tough even for the rich.

Both girls were good-looking but Granny was the prettier of the two. Nellie was six years older and very independent for the times.

My grandmother was always formal with us and never gave us any personal insights into her life experiences. I remember only the story of when Nellie dragged her across the North Country moors. After walking for hours, Granny was relieved when Nellie finally allowed her to rest her blistered feet. But Nellie announced there was still time to walk a further ten miles. Nellie went to Germany to polish her piano playing at the Leipzig Conservatoire of Music. After Leipzig, she travelled around the world working as a governess to rich families first in Seattle and then Honolulu. Elsie left Saltburn at sixteen and was sent to Switzerland. She spent two years at a finishing school near Montreux. When we were young, Granny would make remarks in French at the table when she didn't want us to understand. Elsie returned home in 1911. Soon after Nellie also came home from her travels to look after their mother.

Thomas and Mary Walton had vacated the Willows, which became the home of The Colonel and his new wife Olive. They moved to a large house, not quite finished at the beginning of the war. The house, Dortmund, had been built for Paul and Nora Schwarz, great friends of the Waltons and the Hares, until August 1914. They were Germans and so interned for the duration of the war. Thomas had invested a great deal of money in the house, having put in all the fine oak woodwork. So he bought it. As the Saxe-Coburgs changed their name to Windsor, so Dortmund became Uplands.

## Trevor's Cousin George and a trip to the Far East

After Elsie's marriage and the death of their mother, Mary Walton, in 1918, Nellie continued to keep house for her father at Uplands. She also became involved in helping to run the household of a Scottish widower who lived locally with his children. Dr George Yuille Caldwell had been born in Kilmarnock in 1879. On leaving school he had worked as an apprentice to a pharmacist in Birkenhead until a local doctor noticed his aptitude and paid for his medical education at Glasgow University. He qualified as a doctor. Then in 1905, he took an eight-month trip to the Far East.

During the sea voyage, he corresponded with an Elsie Lake who came from Plymouth, by sending her postcards along the way. They later married and settled in Crook where Dr Caldwell bought Meadow House and a medical practice. They had two children. Douglas was born in 1909 and Jean in 1911 but then in 1915 Elsie died. Nellie was now in her early thirties and in risk of being 'left on the shelf'. The young men she might have wanted to marry were either dead or far afield in the dominions. Dr Caldwell was in need of a wife and she was in need of a husband. So, there was a wedding.

There was a black-and-white photograph of the wedding party. They were a group of dour-looking folk in black silk hats and morning coats arranged outside the conservatory at Uplands. Nellie looked very smart in a huge white hat with osprey feathers. After the wedding, Dr Caldwell, and his children, moved to live with his new wife at Uplands. They had two children together: Harry born in 1921 and George four years later in December 1924. Dr Caldwell was fond of his malt whisky and one of Nellie's challenges during the years of the next war was to procure his daily dram.

Dr Caldwell spoke with a thick Glaswegian accent. There was no conversation at the breakfast table and little at other times. The children were told that they were not to disturb him. While their father was in the house, the children were sent outside to play. The weather had to be extraordinarily bad for them to be allowed to stay indoors. It was often wet and windy. They had bicycles though and plenty of rough land to explore nearby. When the tubs (bringing the coal out of the drift mines close by) started rolling at half-past eleven, they knew that it was time to head back home for lunch.

Dr Caldwell was reputed to be a good doctor but his son, George junior, felt no natural inclination for medicine. In 1943, when he went along to enlist in the navy, George thought he had escaped. Coming home that evening, in the morning room were his Uncle Fred (the Colonel) and his Mama looking very glum and disheartened. This was natural since there had been so many deaths of friends and family in the First War. But his father was not in the least concerned, so George went. While George was away in the navy, his father died. On his return, George told his mother of his intention to study architecture. But Nellie stopped the car and said,

*"One of the things your father said before he died was, 'Get those two buggers through Medicine and then they can do what the hell they like!'"* George's father had little capital and he, no doubt, thought the medical profession would provide a good living.

After qualifying, George spent an initial five years in a country practice in Yorkshire. Then looking on the map for the place furthest removed from County Durham, he set off on a ship for Singapore. George arrived in Singapore in the late 1950s when there was still British colonial rule (until 1965). Over the following decades, he saw Singapore grow in prosperity. George bought an apartment and there were often cranes visible from his apartment on the eighteenth floor. Just by looking out at the changing landscape from his apartment window, George could indulge his life-long interest in architecture. His neighbours were ambassadors and the like. He enjoyed a sociable life through gentlemen's clubs, the excellent restaurants of the city and visits to the opera. He lived well and Trevor, envious of his lifestyle, liked to call him King George! George travelled frequently especially in the Far East and was well-informed about the history and politics of the region.

In 1972, when I was eleven, Trevor decided to take us out to the Far East while I still qualified for a child fare. During the long flight, I noted how easily he talked to strangers, both the flight attendants and fellow passengers. Trevor was a good conversationalist and got on well with women. He had the easy charm of actors like Roger Moore and Cary Grant. After arriving in Singapore, George came to meet us at the airport in his chauffeur-driven black Mercedes. Domestic labour was cheap so George employed a maid, a cook as well as a chauffeur. George later confided that his Malay chauffer had banned him from driving the car after he had a small accident.

We stayed at a hotel near George's apartment. Sarah and I had a room on the ground floor that faced onto the pool. Trevor had a room a little further along. Sarah and I felt like millionaires. We swam in the large contoured pool every day. It was so warm that we went swimming at midnight. Trevor even bought us some goggles. One day George took us for a trip around some of the small islands close to Singapore on his speed boat. Sarah and I collected exotic shells on the white sand beach of one of the islands. On another day, George served us with a very grand high tea in his apartment.

George arranged for us to stay with friends of his, who lived on a rubber plantation in Malaysia. We took a bus to Kota Tinggi and experienced Asia proper for the first time. Dad bought some sugar cane from a seller for us to try. The humidity, the exotic smells, the tropical vegetation and the villages along the way made a lasting impression. They were all so different to what we were used to. George's friends lived in a spacious house on a rubber estate. I was fascinated to see the rubber trees with the little pots collecting the sap. We watched the Malay workers making latex in the factory. We had learned about rubber at school so it was interesting to see that the real thing was just like the pictures in our school textbooks.

After Singapore, we flew to Bangkok. Close to the hotel there was a street market in one of the squares and we looked around the stalls. Sarah and I enjoyed playing with some puppies for sale. Afterwards, someone Trevor met in a bar warned him that it was possible to get rabies from these animals. The time we enjoyed most was spent in the hotel pool. There were bananas on the trees beside the pool and we learned that they grow upwards. Taxis were unbearably hot and we were too young to appreciate sightseeing trips. However, one trip we did enjoy was taking a ride on a small boat upriver to the floating market. We were fascinated by the little monkeys and we fed a baby elephant. In the hotel lobby, Trevor saw a gold ring for sale. It was shaped like a snake with a jewel embedded in its flattened head. I knew it was expensive because he delayed a few days before finally buying it. One evening Trevor took us to see the film South Pacific because it was set in Thailand.

Trevor introduced us to a young Thai man called Hans who was to accompany us on our trip to the beach resort of Pattaya. Dad rented a couple of small huts for a few nights. We ate our meals together. Sarah and I played together most of the day. Sometimes Hans spent some time with us. I was fascinated by the Thai language and script. I asked Hans to write down some simple words for me. Years later, I continued this interest by learning to write Japanese characters. Our last stop was Hong Kong and we flew in over the harbour. Sarah had been moved up to first class because there was no more economy seating on the Jumbo jet. A fellow passenger told her about the wreak of the ocean liner The Queen Elizabeth, which had caught fire and still lay in Hong Kong Harbour at the time.

It was after this trip that Trevor and George became good friends. Trevor made many trips out to the Far East and benefited from George's contacts. We saw George from time to time on one of his annual visits. He used to stay a few nights in London. Then Trevor would drive him up North as far as Scotland to see Derry Baird. Derry was a tall, shy Scot and an old school friend of Trevor's. Whilst in Durham, George stayed at The County Hotel. He liked the comfort of a hotel room as well as a quiet refuge from other people's homes. He and Trevor were entertained in style by Barbara and Alastair while in Durham. I used to look on enviously at these family gatherings because ironically, I missed the family support that George and my father had been so eager to escape.

## Trevor's youth and failing his medical studies

My father, Samuel Trevor Hare, was born in April 1920. As a boy, his bedroom was often cluttered with some creative hobby he was working on. He liked projects that involved building things. He had trains at one time. He also made model ships out of wood from his father's carpentry. These models had no working parts. Unlike his father, Trevor was interested in the artistic effect rather than in engineering. He used pins, cotton and bits of card. The model ships were placed in a coastal landscape that he built. Trevor was a dreamer rather than a doer. In later life, I noted he always paid for someone else to change a car tyre and do his decorating for him.

Frank got on well with his daughter but his relationship with his son was more problematic. They were opposites. Frank was a keen sportsman and a traditional man fond of practical hobbies. Trevor preferred talking. So he was often more comfortable in the company of women. As a boy, his ambition was to be a chef on one of the long-distance Pullman trains. Trevor became interested in cooking because of the time he spent in the kitchen watching his mother cook. She was a good cook and he learned from her. This came in useful later because he was a bachelor for most of his life.

Being able to cook presentable meals, allowed Trevor to entertain his friends and to enjoy the sociable aspects of his personality.

My father was sent first to Bow School as a weekly boarder and then later to Durham School as a day boy. Trevor was unhappy at school especially when he was boarding. It was customary in those days for a son to take up his father's profession. So it was assumed, as a matter of course, that Trevor would become a doctor. In 1937 Trevor embarked on his medical education at King's College, Newcastle. But at the age of twenty, he contracted meningitis. This could have been fatal but fortunately they were able to save his life. A cure, called Sulphonamides (Czechoslovakia, in 1935), had just been discovered. After this Trevor struggled with his exams even with the extra private tuition paid for by his parents. In the end he got stuck on the fourth-year pathology exam, which he kept failing.

Years later Barbara blamed her brother's failure to qualify as a doctor on the meningitis. She told us that some of the after-effects of meningitis include poor mental concentration and an inability to retain facts. She was always quick to defend her brother. She was determined that circumstances had stood against him including the fact that his twin brother had died at birth. Even when she told the story of how, as children, Trevor used to take her toys and demand that she paid him to get them back, she laughed. Despite his lack of career success, Barbara was convinced of Trevor's intelligence and she told us that he was known as 'the professor' at school.

George followed Trevor to Newcastle five years later and his view was that Trevor played around too much. My own impression was that he had no interest in Medicine. Despite his many years of medical training, I never once heard my father make a single reference to any medical knowledge. Nor did he display any technical knowledge of any topic. He was not remotely academic. George came back from his three years' National Service in 1946, just as Trevor was joining the Navy. When Trevor resumed his studies, he still could not get past the Pathology final, by which time George was ahead of him and left in 1951. More than ten years after he started, Trevor finally dropped out of medical school and moved away from his parent's home in the North to live in London.

For the first time in his life and free of parental control, in London Trevor lived life to the full. He enjoyed a sociable and promiscuous lifestyle. He knew many radio and stage personalities and had many affairs. Trevor drove a sports car and had a flat in the upmarket Mayfair. All of this was paid for by his parents. He didn't need to work but it was expected that he should. One of his first jobs was as a clerk for a shipping agency. George Caldwell told me: *"He moved to London and after acting host in various night-clubs, Ciro's was one I think, he acted a part in the 'Arctic Theatre' at the 1951 Festival of Britain on the South Bank. Across the stage with snow blowing a blizzard he would crack his whip and drive a team of huskies as he cried "Mooosh!" He ran a theatre restaurant with a friend for some time then it became boring."*

Trevor eventually settled at BOAC where he worked for thirteen years as a check-in clerk at the central London terminal building in Victoria. The travel industry suited his lifestyle. He enjoyed the people and the discounted travel perks. Obtaining custody of two children provided the ideal excuse for ending his employment. He could now say that he was retired, which sounded quite respectable. In truth, he had never enjoyed the limitations and the daily routine of employment. He now decided to live off his rental income.

*George Caldwell wrote: "I told you the story of his arrival in Penang, I think? Maybe not. Chris worked there for two or three years in the early Seventies. Your Dad would adventure upon the Thai Railroad and came slowly down from Bangkok to Butterworth, opposite Penang on the mainland and Chris would meet him, not having seen him ever before. So, I briefed him as best I could. I said he was an inch or so taller than I and had more or less the same but nicer looks. That he might be dressed rather extravagantly and colourfully. He often was. Maybe in short shorts. Coloured scarf. He would have to be open minded.*

*When the train stopped, out stepped a rather outrageously dressed figure with a Florida hat and scarf, and some jewellery too. Your Pa was quite distressed and rather taken aback to see Christopher go up to this flamboyant American who had been such a nuisance all the way down from Bangkok, and address him "Are you Mr. Hare?" Mr. Hare himself of course was impeccably dressed as though ready to lunch at Harrods' Georgian Room! But they got on famously and later, of course, Chris came to lodge with you at Gaspar Close for the year or so he worked in the West End."*

## My aunt Barbara and the Turnbull family

My aunt Barbara was born in July 1925. They were an affluent family and the children were undoubtedly indulged. Granny lectured them on the need to respect that other people (such as their domestic staff) did not have so many nice things. Barbara was a pretty and likeable girl. Both parents must have idolised her. Barbara liked to travel with her father in his Riley around his practice. She admired her father and consequently the medical profession. With the outbreak of war in 1939, her parents were worried that the east coast of England might be shelled, as had happened in the Great War. They decided to send Barbara, aged fourteen, to Howells, a boarding school in North Wales. She was there for four years before going on to study Pure Science at Durham University. But Barbara wanted to join the war effort. She decided to abandon her degree after one year and enter the navy. She joined other WRNS recruits in London, where she stayed long enough to narrowly escape being hit by a doodlebug bomb.

When Barbara received her orders, she was told to report to the Admiralty in Bath, in the West Country, where she drove *"anything from a sack of potatoes to an Admiral and anything from an Austin 7 to a five-ton truck"*. Granny had always been a good driver and her daughter shared her love of driving. Barbara had learned to drive in her mother's Riley, a luxury motor car with pre-select gears. Now she had to use manual gears. The war ended in 1945 and Barbara proudly joined the Victory parade in London before returning home. Foreign travel was possible once more. Barbara accompanied her parents on a holiday to Canada, crossing the Atlantic both ways on luxury liners, the Queen Elizabeth and the Queen Mary. In 1946 Barbara met Alastair Turnbull, the son of family friends and two years later they became engaged.

Then in 1950, aged 25, Barbara suffered a serious fit. She had suffered a similar attack while away at school when she was fifteen. Frank called the best neurologist in the North East. That same evening Barbara was in the Royal Victoria Infirmary in Newcastle under the care of Professor Henry Miller. She had to lie flat for six weeks and was forbidden to move. When she recovered, Barbara was sent to see Sir Charles Symonds, the neurologist and Wylie McKissock (later knighted), the neurosurgeon. After tests, they confirmed that she had what they described as a berry aneurism on the brain. Her condition was called angiomata, which can cause subarachnoid haemorrhaging. Blood leaks into the brain from the many tiny blood vessels on the Circle of Willis feeding the brain.

Gradually each attack (leakage of blood) was removing more and more of her field of vision. Given time it could render her blind. It might even prove fatal. It had recently been discovered that the condition was operable but Symonds and McKissock decided to do nothing for the time being. There was a possibility she might never have another attack. If she did, Barbara would need to have surgery. The specialists gave their blessing for the marriage to go ahead. With some trepidation, Barbara and Alastair were married on 2nd June 1951. Everything went well until September 1952 when the young couple were holidaying in a caravan in Scotland.

Barbara had another attack. Ignoring reassurances from the local doctor, Alastair called his father-in-law. A few hours later Frank's Bentley pulled up outside and Elsie stepped out exclaiming *"I have NEVER come around Loch Lomond so fast in my life!"* Frank advised staying put for another week before heading home. Once home, Barbara had to lie flat on her back for another six weeks. Brain surgery was still in its infancy. A major operation of this kind was only offered by the John Radcliffe Infirmary (Oxford) or the National Hospital (London). It was a formidable operation and Barbara was pregnant. They decided she should have her baby first.

Barbara's son John was born in February 1953. In September, Barbara (aged 28) set off for London, leaving her son with her mother. She wondered whether she would ever see him again. The surgery left her with a 180-degree field of vision in both eyes so that she was effectively blind on the left side. The medical term was 'a complete left homonymous hemianopia'. Barbara explained this as normal sight on a clock face from 12 noon to 6 pm but blind in both eyes from 6pm back to 12. The definition was so close that once Barbara had written the capital 'B' for her name and moved on to the 'a', she could no longer see the 'B'. It was to be 8 years before the blurred vision cleared and she could see properly again (albeit with this blackout on her left-hand-side vision in both eyes).

Barbara's daughter Susan was born in March 1956. During Barbara's absence, Granny had employed a nanny called Mary to help care for her young grandson. Mary agreed to stay on until Barbara had recovered from Sue's birth. Alastair was fond of shooting so there were often birds to be plucked and gutted. Dinner preparations could take up much of the day. John went to boarding school at the age of seven and Sue lost her playmate. In the holidays, John no longer wanted to play with his baby sister. When her time came, Sue went to boarding school in tears. Later Sue told me of her carefree memories of The Sneep. Coming from a stable home she had not suffered my shyness and insecurities. She was also sporty and enjoyed games all the way through her school days.

My Aunt Barbara's operation left her with a scar on the brain, which meant that she was prone to epileptic fits. This condition did not manifest itself for 18 months but thereafter Barbara had to take daily anticonvulsant drugs for the rest of her life. Unfortunately, Barbara was very forgetful and she suffered many attacks of epilepsy between 1955 and 1963. Each time Barbara found herself in the increasingly familiar surroundings of the RVI in Newcastle. After two or three such episodes of forgetfulness, Henry Miller advised her in his avuncular manner from the foot of her hospital bed: *"... and, for Christ's sake, take those bloody pills!"*

Barbara continued to forget to take her pills with her when she left the house, especially if they left in a hurry. This naturally caused some considerable inconvenience to the only driver in the house. One time they left in a hurry and Barbara had to summon up the courage to break the news. On telling him, Alastair simply turned the car around. She, like the chastised schoolgirl, went sheepishly back into the house to fetch her pill box. In relating such stories Barbara made light of how intimidating Alastair's temper could be.

Barbara and Alastair had embarked on married life in a terraced house in Chester-le-Street but Barbara had her ambition set on a larger stone-built house a few miles south on the road to Durham. As a child, Barbara had often noticed the house called The Grove at Plawsworth. It was right by the side of the main road between Durham and Chester-le-Street. She decided that she would like to live there when she grew up. The house came up for sale and the young couple went to view it. They decided to buy it and spent many years refurbishing it to create a comfortable family home.

The household in which Alastair had grown up was anything but harmonious. Family disagreements were openly aired and opinions volubly expressed. The Hare household was quite different, more formal and much calmer, with little raising of voices. So, Barbara was not used to a domestic atmosphere of army camp swearing. Early in their marriage after an argument, Barbara stormed off pettishly to the bedroom and locked the door. After a pause, a contrite Alastair came to the door and, adopting a cajoling Geordie accent, negotiated a reconciliation *"Ee come on, pet... Are you all right? I'm sorry, ... I didn't mean it."* Barbara could not resist his sense of humour and his boyish charm. And so they carried on.

Alastair was the son of Jack Turnbull, another colonel. He and my father's Uncle Fred (the Colonel) got on well together gurrumphing at each other over their whisky. Alastair volunteered as a private in the army on his 18th birthday and served in the seventh Armoured Division of the British Army of the Rhine in Germany. After his release from the army in 1947, Alastair joined the Territorial Army 8th Battalion DLI until 1954 with the honorary rank of Captain. In his younger days, Alastair had been an accomplished cricketer as well as a boxer. Despite his shorter build, rugby was the game where he excelled. Barbara and Alastair were a sociable couple and they often invited guests to the house for dinner. They were both fond of telling stories, jokes and anecdotes. Alastair's repertoire of jokes included those he had accumulated from years of rugby and TA dinners. Alastair's jokes, even when selected for polite company, were considerably more bawdy than we were used to. My parents never told jokes. Later Alastair also served as a local Justice of the Peace, presiding over petty crime cases in the magistrates' court.

Alastair's older brother Ian was killed in the Second World War. So after the war, Alastair took over the family land-agency business from his father. Jack Turnbull was a difficult man and a strict father. While working together, father and son communicated via their secretary. The head office was in Chester-le-Street with satellite offices in neighbouring towns. There was a residential side to the business with shopfronts but Alastair looked after the land agency work. He advised private clients on the management of their moors and estates. He organised shoots and managed the estate staff. The grouse season starts on The Glorious Twelfth (of August), once the young birds are independent. Amateur shots found that shooting wild birds was not as easy as it looked. Sarah and I naturally viewed shooting as a pastime for the rich. Alastair explained that checking the growth in the bird population ensured that all would have enough to eat. This is part of moor maintenance just as the controlled burning of the old heather allows new shoots to grow.

One of Alastair's most prestigious clients was the Earl of Strathmore who appointed Alastair as his agent in the mid-1960s. My uncle managed the Strathmore estates in County Durham, including Holwick, a shooting lodge and extensive estate at Middleton in Teesdale. The King of Spain was among the guests invited by the Strathmores but others came as paying guests. Since the estate belonged to the Bowes-Lyon family, the Queen Mother, H.M. Queen, Charles and Philip all visited in the season. Barbara was invited to accompany her husband on some social occasions. Alastair respected the institution as well as the personalities but he knew his place. Alastair was respected and when he died in 2001, the Strathmore family took an early train from Dundee to get down in time for his funeral service. At his father's memorial service, John Turnbull said *"My father was a good man and a kind father. He was my mother's rock, caring for her without reserve for many years. Tough but not hard. Full of humour, a great raconteur."*

## Holidays with Trevor and his family in the North

Trevor continued to live in the house in Battersea. In the holidays, we slept in a spare room on the ground floor. The other floors were let. I used to lie awake in bed at night listening to the songs Trevor liked from musicals such as My Fair Lady and The Sound of Music. One night when I could not sleep, he gave me a tot of cherry brandy and talked to me about the stock exchange. When I was a child, I couldn't imagine that I would ever have the experience and knowledge of adults. Trevor's talk of basic economics inspired me later to take up a finance career. Occasionally Trevor entertained friends. He liked to showcase his culinary skills with ambitious dishes like cheese soufflé but then he worried that it would collapse before his guests arrived. One of Trevor's friends, Ted Barnes, who lived nearby was a wine buyer. Trevor taught us how to play Canasta and some evenings Ted would come to make up the foursome. Sarah and I liked him because he was always cheerful and chatty.

Towards the end of our time at The Sneep, Trevor moved from Battersea to a mews house off the Gloucester Road in the West End of London not far from Harrods. The flat had three floors with an open staircase and there was a roof garden. The house was brighter and more modern in its layout and decoration than the house in Battersea. Trevor bought a four-poster bed that had been a prop in the film Mary Queen of Scots so we had to go and see the film again. Trevor told us that he was thinking of having a lodger, as we were there so little. Trevor often had friends visiting. Mary occasionally appeared. She was quite a character and had a good sense of humour. I was embarrassed by Mary's habit of talking and laughing loudly in public places. Once we all went down to Brighton in the Brighton Belle train to visit the Royal Pavilion.

Two middle-aged women lived together in one of the other houses in the mews at Gloucester Road. Rita and Geraldine were typical of the idiosyncratic people Trevor knew in London. A friend of Geraldine's was a fashion journalist for The Daily Telegraph newspaper. She invited Sarah and I to go along with her to see a fashion show. We sat behind the scenes and watched the models changing. I was fascinated to watch these women applying make-up and pulling on their nylons and high-heeled shoes. Jo had neither the money nor the interest to be fashionable. So this was the first time that I experienced the impact of the feminine beauty industry.

As a retired employee, Trevor was entitled to cheap travel on a standby basis both on BOAC's long-distance flights and more recently also on BEA's short-haul flights. British Airways was formed from the merger of the two national carriers in 1974. He used to send us postcards at school from different parts of the world: Australia, San Francisco, Switzerland and the Far East among others. We were also entitled to discounted tickets. These cost 5% of the full fare until we were twelve when the cost rose to the adult standby fare of 10%. Trevor loved travelling. He wanted to inspire us so we would enjoy travelling when we were adults.

When I was ten Trevor took Sarah and me to Italy. We started in Rome but the city was hot. Trevor seemed disappointed that we were not interested in seeing the sights. We took a train up the coast to La Spezia and stayed in a hotel by the sea. The taxi driver overcharged us on the journey from the station. Later Trevor was overjoyed when we got the same driver for the return trip. He took great delight in underpaying him to compensate for the previous excess. Even if it was warranted, I remember that his jubilation embarrassed me. The sea water was warm and I decided that I should learn to swim, which I did. Sarah and I played in the pool together while Trevor read a book. I thought it was the height of decadence to order bottles of real fruit juice to drink by the pool.

After this trip to Italy, Feri and I invented our own Italiano language. We already had to learn French and Latin at school. So the idea of learning a real language (like Italian) held little appeal. We liked the idea of having a means of communicating without anyone understanding us. Certainly our code infuriated at least one matron, who retaliated by calling us babyish. We built the language up slowly. Whenever we needed a new word, we invented one. Soon Feri and I had a vocabulary of a few hundred words and we were able to express the simple things children say very fluently.

We devised a simple grammar based on the languages we already knew, primarily English. The experience has helped me understand how languages evolve. I realised that vocabulary evolves continuously through the spoken language. But no population can spontaneously decide on a logical structure of grammar rules. A grammar must be devised by people who appreciate the need for more precise communication. They then educate others. This is done through the written language which is more easily controlled. Over time these grammar rules are corrupted by various exceptions as people use the language for daily spoken communication.

Once we started at the Sneep, each holiday began and ended with at least one day spent at my grandmother's house. On our long car journeys travelling back and forth, I always sat in the front. I was older than Sarah but also, I suffered from car sickness in the back. In any case, I was much more talkative than Sarah. Trevor enjoyed talking to a captive and admiring audience. Despite turning his back on traditional values, he told us of the importance of marriage and career. Perhaps this is one of the hypocrisies of being a parent that we set goals for our children what we could not achieve ourselves.

After Grandpa died, The Close was much too big for Granny on her own. She moved to a small bungalow in Chester-le-Street, near to the town and the shops. She was now having difficulty walking. Initially she used walking sticks but later she needed a wheelchair. Frances came as a daily help and for a short while Granny employed a live-in companion. We had to improvise our own amusements. In 1971 we spent Christmas with Trevor at Granny's house. I was ten and it was the last Christmas we spent away from Jo. Trevor gave me a large teddy bear and a week-to-a-page diary. This started my hobby of keeping a daily diary for the next six years.

We were spending less and less time at Granny's house now that she was confined to a wheelchair. For a more active household, Sarah and I visited Aunty Barbara. Once we even walked the 2 miles along the dual carriageway. We enjoyed our visits because Barbara was entertaining and cheerful. My aunt spent most of her day in the kitchen preparing one meal or other. She was often engaged in preparing game, usually grouse or a partridge, from one of Alastair's shooting expeditions. Barbara showed us how she plucked, gutted and prepared the bird for roasting in the oven.

Their front door was only used on formal occasions. The daily entrance was around the side and led through a lobby cloakroom directly into the kitchen, the heart of the house. The kitchen had a low ceiling, a farmhouse-style stone floor and an oil-fired Aga stove. Past the kitchen there was a playroom where the family watched television in front of the open log fire. Both the playroom and the dining room had polished wooden floorboards and rugs. Past the dining room was the lobby, the front door and the stairs to the bedrooms. The drawing room, at the far end of the house, was a formal room and although carpeted, often chilly and unused.

I used to go there because it was where the piano was kept. I would sneak away to pick out my favourite tunes with one finger. Occasionally Barbara played for me. I loved to watch her hands moving over the piano keys as she played from memory: Leibestraum, elegant waltzes and songs from old musicals. Despite my early interest in the piano, no one ever suggested that we should learn. On our visits, Barbara entertained us with explanations of her disability as well as stories from her everyday life. She told us how her earlier brain surgery had affected her sight and described the dangers of getting about with her disability. She had to give up driving in 1953. Apart from her shopping trips into Newcastle on the bus, her life was restricted to the house and kitchen. Whether on the bus or in the shops, Barbara enjoyed engaging fellow passengers, shopkeepers and other shoppers in political debate.

Barbara was a colourful character. She could be as imperious as Granny but she was more approachable. She had an unfailing ability to see the amusing side of life and a wonderful giggle. At breakfast my aunt and uncle sat around the breakfast table, each with a newspaper, commenting on topical issues. They were both active in local politics especially during electioneering. Barbara enjoyed reminiscing about the war years, particularly the food rationing and the positive morale of the British population. It often seemed to Sarah and me that the Second World War had just ended. Barbara echoed the politics of her parents' class, the Tories.

My Uncle Alastair always kept a gun dog, a black Labrador. There was also a fierce-looking Yorkshire terrier who used to sit on the kitchen armchair. We were told to give her a wide berth. She would snap and growl at us if we went near her. They also kept a couple of cats. Long after she had died, we were told the story of Mrs Pierson, one of their cats. Mrs Pierson had been an acquaintance who had a gap between her two front teeth. She spoke with a whistle that Barbara enjoyed mimicking with a good-natured chuckle.

Sarah and I were often aware of the tension in the household. We had little experience of this kind of relationship standoff or indeed any other aspect of marital life. Neither of my parents had the stress of a career and they were both single. So I was rarely exposed to the typical gender roles men and women assume in marriage. Our cousin Sue, who was five years older than me, grew up helping out in the kitchen in the family tradition for women. Compared with my own family, the expectations seemed old-fashioned but probably they were typical. We interacted little with John, who was eight years older than me and a man by now. I remember being impressed that he could do the cryptic crossword in the Telegraph. Trevor only ever did the easy one and even that was beyond me.

My aunt's home help, Mrs Dawson, had been the office cleaner for my uncle's business before she came to help Barbara in the house and to look after her two small children. Growing up with a much less formal family, I found it strange that these two women always addressed each other as Mrs Turnbull and Mrs Dawson despite knowing each other for nearly 30 years. Barbara looked on Mrs Dawson as "a confidante and wonderful friend" during the years when she had little other adult companionship. Sarah and I thought her a little scary. She was a short woman with sharp-looking eyes and a quick tongue. We couldn't understand her Geordie accent.

Eventually Barbara and Alastair had an annex built onto the side of The Grove, next to the kitchen, so that Granny could live with them. Granny never talked about her life but she did show us photos of her at school in Montreux. She used to play cards with us occasionally. Bezique and New Market were favourites of hers. Barbara enjoyed having daily contact with her mother. Granny was more intellectual and informed about the world. Barbara tried to pick up tips for managing her financial affairs. When Trevor visited, they made up a comfortable threesome. Trevor shared upper class values and a sense of humour with his mother and sister. They liked to tell and re-tell stories from the past. The closeness between mother and son was also evident to me through their letters. After one of his visits, Granny wrote (31st January 1980): *"Daddy rang up from the airport last night to say he was on his way. I felt that I was losing a friend."* My grandmother died in 1983. Up to the end she had Barbara, Trevor and Sue visiting. Even Sarah went to see her, while she was hospitalised in Durham.

# PART IV: MY ADOLESCENCE

## The transition from prep school to senior school

In September 1972 I arrived back at the Sneep for my last year. Our form teacher was Miss McConchie, who always took the senior class. Everyone said that I was teacher's pet because she seemed to favour me. Nevertheless, I was often in trouble for losing something. *"Conkers blew me up"* or *"Mrs H blew me up"* were common entries in my diary. Everyone was talking about their senior schools. The natural choice for me would have been Queen Margaret's School, Harrogate, where my cousin Sue went after the Sneep. But Sue had not been happy at Queen Margaret's. Behind the scenes and unknown to us, Jo had been asking for our senior school to be in the South of England. Feri was going to Queen Anne's School (QAS), a boarding school in Caversham. Granny had been introduced to the Feri's parents and no doubt approved of the connection. She agreed to pay for me to go to QAS with Feri.

Feri's mother had gone to QAS many years before with a scholarship. So Feri and I were both entered for the scholarship. After we had passed the qualification test, we went to Queen Anne's to take the scholarship exams. Perhaps fortunately for our friendship (because we were competitive), neither of us won a scholarship. Once we joined the school, we learned that the scholarship girls got A grades in every subject not just one or two as we did. In our last term at the Sneep, we all had main parts in a senior school play directed by Miss McConchie called The Gentle Rain. The title came from Portia's speech in the Shakespeare play The Merchant of Venice where she pleads with the Jew, Shylock, to show mercy towards her fiancé. I was cast as the Emperor of China, a role I enjoyed. I was all-forgiving towards a miscreant general played by Laura. The play was performed on the last day of term. Trevor came to fetch us and I was pleased he saw the play.

Sarah was still too young to go to QAS so she stayed at The Sneep for another year. This was the first time that Sarah and I had been separated. Sarah became much closer to Granny during this year. I started at Queen Anne's September 1973 when I was twelve. The uniform was a blue tweed skirt and blouse worn with nylon tights in winter, which made me feel very grown up. I was used to wearing woollen tights in winter and long socks in summer. QAS was a big step up in maturity and initially I was intimidated by the other girls who seemed very sophisticated. Within a few weeks though, even I had moved away from my childish games and teddy bears. My first worry was making friends. I was hoping for the kind of popularity I had enjoyed at the Sneep. But this was a much bigger school.

There was a junior boarding house for girls in the lowest year and a senior boarding house for girls in the top year. For the other years, girls were allocated to a house. There were two at the end of the field and two within the school building. Feri and I were in Wilkins which was close to the main building and next door to Webbe. When I arrived back at school, I was often overwhelmed with homesickness and depression. Although we had fun at school, there were also a whole variety of worries and stresses to deal with as well. After holidays spent in Kingsclere, the impersonal dormitories felt like an institution. I learned to deal with my emotions by keeping busy and not dwelling on my feelings. I would unpack, have a bath and get myself organised for school life. By the time everyone had arrived and it was time to go to bed, it seemed as if I had never been away from school. Despite my appreciation of home, I often wrote in my diary that it was *"Great to be back at school"*. School was our base and defined the core of our lives.

On the ground floor of Wilkins, there was a large sitting room, called the common room for us to use during our free time. Here there was a record player, a ping-pong table, casual chairs and sofas and plenty of paperbacks to read. The lower sixth had their own study as well as a TV room where they could watch television more freely than the junior girls could. The juniors had to go across to the dining room in the adjacent house and sit on the long tables to watch television. At the beginning of term, each year group had to agree on three programmes they wanted to watch each week. I took little interest in the choice as it hardly seemed worth the bother. One of the programmes was always Top of the Pops. Otherwise the girls chose popular TV series that were running at the time.

Water fights were common and difficult to cover up if matron or the house mistress, Miss Leahy or Leeks as we called her, walked in. *"We got caught with the lights on, revising. Went down to Leeks. Had to stand in the dark in different rooms for half an hour!"* Once when we were caught, we had to strip our beds, remake them and then copy lines from a book. Our misdoings at school were all quite innocent. Occasionally the more daring girls used to creep out of the house at night and meet up with girls from houses in the old school building. There were tunnels under the quadrangle, which they knew how to get into. The idea of creeping along narrow tunnels in the dark did not appeal to me. I didn't want to get trapped in these old tunnels, which were partly collapsed.

One morning I was on my bed humming. Vicky threw talc over me to shut me up, which ended up in a talc fight. All my clothes were covered in talc and so were hers. Di came in from the loo and we decided to attack her. She refused to use her own talc to pay us back and there was an outcry when she started using other people's talc. Next, she went and got water in her cup but we ran downstairs and the buzzer for lunch went. After lunch, I did not want to go up and get soaked so I did some ironing. We often had water fights because there were two washbasins in the larger dorm of six beds. It was very easy to fill a tooth mug and then throw it at someone. Once we had a butter fight after which I had to wash butter out of my hair. The main motivation for these fights was to have fun but they were also a test of how far we could go with each other.

In the upper fifth, someone discovered black magic. In the dark after lights out, we put a glass on a mirror and each put a finger on the glass. After a while, it would start moving around. I assumed it was because of static electricity but the idea was that spirits were causing the glass to move. I joined in despite my scepticism. With Christmas coming there were decorations to be put up in the dorm. We made these from toilet paper. Miss Leahy was a piano teacher as well as the choir mistress. On the last evening of the Christmas term, the whole house sang Christmas carols in the house mistress's sitting room. There was hot Ribena, with peanuts and mince pies.

Occasionally I enjoyed school life so much that I temporarily forgot about all my worries and insecurities. We finished the term with a midnight feast and a water fight. Sometimes each year group was asked to prepare a short piece of entertainment (called a house skit) for an informal house show performed in the common room. I was self-conscious about acting especially if comedy was involved. The others were impatient and laughed at me. I felt depressed the whole evening. In the end, everything went wrong and I enjoyed myself.

Later that year the house put on a performance of the 1920's musical The Boyfriend. The main parts went to the senior girls but I was flattered to be asked to support the singing of a couple of songs that needed a soprano. Jo came with Simon to see one of the performances. Afterwards she took me out of school and we sat on the swings in the playing field in Caversham eating fish and chips.

Returning to school for my second year at QAS I was in the Lower Fifth (LV), which meant that we were senior rather than junior girls. We were now eligible to be promoted onto the privilege list. Once on the List we could go shopping in pairs, either walking down into Caversham or catching the bus to Reading. Non-lists could only go shopping on three Saturdays each term but they were not allowed out of school in the week. From this point on being de-listed was the main punishment. I was very pleased to be one of the first girls in my year promoted to the list. I recognised that this was largely due to my reluctance to be involved in any adventurous activities.

Each day we walked over to the main school building for chapel and lessons. When the teacher came into the classroom we had to stand in silence until we were asked to sit. We had free time in the afternoons except on Wednesdays and Saturdays, when we played sport. Each evening there were lessons and homework, which was called prep. The school day went on until 7 pm when there was a hot supper such as toad-in-the-hole (sausages baked in batter) or bubble and squeak (potato and cabbage fried with onion). I enjoyed the food especially the cooked breakfast and the puddings. We said a short grace "for what we are about to receive, may the Lord make us truly thankful" standing at the table before each meal except for tea, to which we helped ourselves in the dining room. We ate loaves of ready sliced white bread with chocolate spread or just white sugar sprinkled on butter. There were various varieties of cheap runny jams, strawberry or apricot and peanut butter, which I detested.

I was no good at anything sporty, which was a severe disadvantage in a public school where we had to play competitive games almost every day. At Queen Anne's the main winter team sport was lacrosse. I had never heard of it before and it was a little unnerving at first that the other girls all knew how to play. A lacrosse stick is a similar length to a hockey stick and has a triangular net at the end. A player catches the ball, roughly the size of a tennis ball, in the net before throwing it on to the next player. To prevent the ball falling out of the net as the player is running along, there is a technique for cradling the ball. Needless to say, I never exactly mastered this sport and spent most of my time either in goal or ineffectually in some defence position out on the wings of the game. Tackling was aggressive and holding onto the ball involved dodging the other players. Even when I was goalie, I jumped out of the way, as a taller heavier girl thundered towards me to shoot the ball into the net.

It often rained and I would stand on the pitch with my glasses steamed up or covered with rain drops and wonder how I was supposed to be gaining anything from the miserable experience. Each week we had to rub the leather struts of the lacrosse stick net with some smelly grease to ensure that the leather did not dry out. The nets became dirty with use and I do not remember what happened to mine when I left school. I wrote in my diary *"Field was absolutely freezing. My feet felt like blocks of ice. I thought I might be able to break my toes off!"* If I had even the hint of a cold, I tried to get off games by getting a written note from matron.

## The onset of puberty and surviving teenage crushes

Sarah joined me at Queen Anne's at the start of my second year. I was proud of my little sister. My friends thought she looked very small and sweet. At the Sneep, Sarah and I had often played together as part of the small group of boarders but at QAS this changed. Sarah was eleven when she started at QAS in the fourth year. This junior year-group lived in a separate house, called Moore. This worked well for Sarah because she made friends with girls who went into other houses later on. I had never had any friendships out of house. Unfortunately though, Sarah was very unhappy during her year in the junior house. Sarah didn't get on well with the matron of Moore, Miss Shorter, known as Shortie.

Although Sarah did not enjoy food as much as I did, she ate most foods now both at The Sneep and at home. Suddenly, her dislike of cheese became a big problem. Sarah told me that Moore was like a prison and how she would sit in the cloakroom in Moore house looking over at Wilkins. She said that she missed me more than anyone else. When I visited, she never wanted me to leave and I felt awful about her being so unhappy. Trevor also felt helpless to solve Sarah's unhappiness. He asked me to see more of Sarah. As a child I usually accepted the authority of adults but also, I would not have had the authority to tell Miss Shorter to leave Sarah alone. I already knew that Trevor never stood up to bullies.

On one occasion I was asked to go to Moore to look after Sarah. She had fainted when the school doctor removed a verruca from her foot. I was shocked that he had used a knife without any form of anaesthetic. I was incredulous that Sarah had let him use a knife on her. At the same time, I was frustrated that I had not been there to protect her. From early childhood, I had seen myself as Sarah's protector but also as her guide. Even when we were with our parents, they did not perform this function. I used to remind Sarah not to lie on the wet grass and to thank people for gifts or having us to stay. I was often treated as the spokesperson for the pair of us. During the holidays, Trevor asked me to talk to Sarah about the problem. He said that Miss Shorter had described her as sullen.

In London, Sarah and I slept on the sofa in the lounge. Sarah asked me to cuddle her and I tried to talk to her about school. But Sarah was unwilling to talk about it. Although she had been unhappy in Moore, Sarah nevertheless benefited from moving into Wilkins already established with her year group. She gained a certain amount of kudos with her friends from the fact that she had a sister in a senior year. Sarah was homesick on a regular basis and I was summoned to comfort her. Over time she came to seek my company less and eventually only asked for me if she was unhappy.

In Moore, Sarah was given the nickname Bunny because of our surname Hare. Later someone told me that a boy with the same surname had been dubbed Pubes. I thought this was a good example of how men like crudeness but women prefer cuteness. Being given an affectionate nickname, was a reflection of Sarah's acceptance by her peers. I was envious because of my insecurities about being viewed as quiet and serious. At school she was called Bunny but at home she was still Sarah. This created a subtle divide between her home and school lives. Despite Sarah's day-to-day independence of me, I always felt obliged to go to her if she asked for me. Rather like the parent-child relationship, the child moves away long before the parent accepts that they are no longer needed.

At QAS there was a system called cracks. A younger girl chose an older girl as a crack. If you were cracked on someone, it meant you admired them. Some of the junior girls could be very silly about their crush and this was often encouraged by the older girl. I was embarrassed about the idea of being involved in this kind of situation. I did not feel inclined to dote on anyone and wondered if I could opt out. Eventually, just to join in, I chose a quiet girl who seemed sensible. I knew that no one else had chosen her and that she might at least have the benefit of the implied compliment. The prime duty of a crack was to spend time chatting by the younger girl's bed on the last night of term. This tradition was called tucking up. I was pleased when my crack turned out to be an interesting and sensible girl who talked easily for the required amount of time.

The following year, I was in the Lower Fifth (LV). Instead of having cracks, we could now potentially be cracks. Although I wanted the ego boost of someone being cracked on me, I also dreaded the self-conscious embarrassment. Nevertheless, I was pleased when Sarah told me that her friend Nicky was cracked on me. Given they were both in the Fourth Form (and hence in Moore House) thankfully I did not have to acknowledge the situation often. My personal confidence was growing and I felt slightly more popular with the other girls. Once I got to the sixth form, I was flattered when a serious and intelligent girl, Alice, chose me as her crack without any silliness. When it came to the last night of term, Alice was not in the least shy and I was relieved to find that she was easy to talk to.

I was often bemused by the other girls' fascination with the opposite sex. They idolised popstars and film stars. Young male visitors were stalked around the grounds. Although I did not know any boys, my interest in reading gave me the impression that I already knew what boys were like. I assumed that they were people in the same way that girls are people. I had no interest in joining the other girls who looked out of the windows at night to see the local boys gathered outside the school walls. Nevertheless, as I progressed through my teens, I became increasingly conscious of my looks. I had always thought of myself as a plain child but I was hoping I might develop into an attractive woman. I had no social life at either of my parent's homes so my only hope of getting to know boys was through school.

My adolescent concerns focused on whether a boy would find me attractive. I was not confident enough to wear revealing clothes. The literature I had read indicated that women who dress provocatively are either selling sex or just being a prick-tease. The words used to describe such women made it clear that they were not respected. I would have been embarrassed to draw attention to myself. Later when I started writing about sexuality, I appreciated the contrast between my own behaviour and the curiosity that adolescent boys have about seeing and touching a girl's body. I had seen my father naked briefly once when I was a child but I did not know exactly what the male genitals looked like. Nevertheless, I had no desire to see a penis either for real or even as an image.

My first memory of puberty was the appearance of some pubic hairs (that were logged initially one at a time!) around the age of 13. It was only through a friend at junior school that I had learned that you were supposed to wash between your legs. No adult ever told me how to wash. Once I had pubic hair, my knickers got wet after urinating if I didn't dry between my legs before pulling up my knickers. Once or twice I tried stroking over my vulva in the bath. I had read about female masturbation and assumed that arousal would be automatic. Evidently it was not. Nothing happened. The experience was such a non-starter that I didn't bother trying again.

When my breasts did finally start growing, I was pleased. My development was so much behind the others (who were also older), that I was relieved to be normal. But I liked my body the way it was as a child so I found this change highly inconvenient. I had always slept on my front. In the initial stages of development, my mammary glands were like small acutely sensitive beads in the centre of each breast. I had to compromise by using my hands to raise my upper body off the bed and avoid crushing my sensitive breasts. The sensitivity wore off over a few months and gradually I became used to this new inconvenience. I wore very flimsy elastic bras initially. Once I got to university, I went to a department store and was amazed when they offered to measure me and provide a fitted bra. I had some very minor stretch marks from the initial growth so I was keen to avoid any more damage to my breasts.

I was starting to wonder when I was going to start my periods. Jo told me that she had been late starting her periods so I assumed that I might be the same. Jo was not coy about her own periods and I saw the packets of tampons she left in the bathroom. I started my periods at the age of 14. My next period occurred almost a year later and after that (from the age of fifteen) they settled into cycle based roughly on 28 days. Initially I used a sanitary pad. This was the simplest solution and involved the least interaction with my genitals, which seemed dirty given the blood. Once my monthly cycle was established, I decided to try the tampons the other girls were using. This was the first time that I was conscious of my vaginal opening. I used the cardboard applicator which came with the tampon inserted inside. It was slightly uncomfortable poking around for the entrance. Another girl told me to put petroleum jelly on the applicator, which helped. Later I used tampons that you insert with a finger. This was easier, more comfortable. Unlike some girls, I was unconcerned about putting a finger into my vagina.

Most girls at school complained of some form of period pains. I never had period pains, stomach cramps, headaches or any other symptoms of pre-menstrual tension (PMT). My mother always referred to periods as the curse but she didn't get period pains either. We got our sex education from articles and readers' letters in Jackie magazine. The information covered menstrual periods, dating boys and other questions adolescent girls have. One holiday, I overheard Trevor talking to Granny about my body changes. I was pleased that he had noticed that I was becoming a woman.

During my years at QAS, I was forever conscious of my inability to talk at any level. I found it difficult to feel at ease with anyone whether my peers, juniors, seniors or staff. I was still self-conscious of my shyness and immaturity. I blamed my lack of social confidence on my family background. Each week Miss Leahy chaired a meeting of the whole house in the common room. The sixth formers assigned marks to the junior girls for posture, grooming and conversation. These were read out during the house meeting. Marks were out of ten, with two or three being a low mark. It did not take long for the seniors to spot my shyness and I always had low marks for conversation. Conversation at mealtimes was much easier once we had exams to talk about. Exams kept us busy and brought us together as a group. We spent a great deal of time preparing to do revision but not much time getting any work done.

On a number of occasions, I had to report to The Study. One time a senior girl lectured me about the need to be more talkative in front of the rest of The Study. I was petrified and humiliated. After that I was acutely aware of the need to make token conversation at the meal table whenever a member of the sixth form was around. A seating plan was put up initially and then we moved one place to the right each meal. So we ended up sitting next to each senior girl in turn because they sat at the ends of the table. On the last week of term, we were allowed to sit next to our friends. It was such a relief for me to enjoy meals without any need to make conversation.

## Learning about relationships by living together

Initially, there were eight other girls in my year group in Wilkins House. Julie, Barley, Jenny, Amanda and Alison were all born in 1960 whereas Feri, Vicky and Diana were born the year before (the same as me). I was friendlier with the girls from the younger group perhaps because of maturity. We took turns pairing up as best friends and daily companion. In the first term, I was in a room with Amanda and Alison. A corridor separated our dormitory from the rest of the girls in our year. After lights-out we had to creep past Matron's room to visit the girls in the larger dorm of six beds. Matron kept her door ajar and it was a challenge to creep along the corridor and past her room without the floorboards creaking.

Miss Heggarty, a tall thin woman with jet black hair, was Irish and had a slightly scatty sense of humour. I have often wondered since whether she accepted a certain amount of fun and games. I am sure she must have heard us. If we were in the other dormitory making too much noise, matron or the house mistress, Leeks, would come into the room and switch the lights on. As the visitors, we had to hide under the beds and hope that we would escape detection. If we were caught, we were marched back to our room in disgrace. It all added to the sense of daring when we next broke the rules.

During exams, some girls would try to fit in extra revision by sitting in the toilet after lights out. One night, Di went to the toilet to read a comic and Heggarty came in wondering where she was. We told her that Di was constipated. Heggarty sat on the bed and chatted to us for a while. She often told quite interesting and amusing stories. Di was gone such a long time that by the time she appeared she had to agree to take one of Heggarty's pills, much to our amusement.

The dormitories had bare wooden floorboards. The iron-framed beds had very firm but thin hammock-shaped mattresses so the only position for sleeping was in the trench. We each had a set of drawers for clothes and a wooden chest at the end of the bed, called a cheeser in which we stored our games kit and shoes. We were allowed a fixed number of items on our drawer top by the bed. Each week we had to move these items onto the bed for the cleaners. School was a routine with intervals of free time. We had a craze on jacks in my first year, which we played on the floor. Pastimes went in phases but playing cards was always popular.

When I got back to school in the summer, I found that I was sharing a dorm with Feri. We had an easy familiarity with each other because of our years spent together. But Feri and I were not as close as when we had been at junior school. Feri had not made new friends as easily as I had. So it was slightly awkward because she was more reliant on our old friendship than I was. Feri told me later *"I could never cope with this going 'on' and 'off' people either at the Sneep or QAS."* Our relationship at The Sneep was founded on playing childish games. Once we became teenagers, talking became more important than playing and the other girls had more to talk about. Feri seemed to lack the confidence to discuss even adolescent issues. I certainly never expected anyone to understand or be able to discuss the issues arising from my family.

Feri told me later: *"After you and I split up as best friends, I was really quite alone on a friendship basis mostly until I moved to Mitchell in Upper Sixth and made two new friends to go about with among the larger crowd. The forced independence of boarding school especially one with such limited opportunities outside the academic was really isolating for someone as shy as I was. I think I must have just retreated inside myself much of the time but there was also the pressure to seem part of the group. With all of you chopping and changing allegiances, I expect I didn't trust you enough to communicate!"*

Of course, it never occurred to me how I might have hurt others. I would not accept rudeness, which I saw as a lack of respect but I was too embarrassed to spell this out. I assumed the transgression was obvious to others but often they were oblivious of the offence. On the other hand, I found that friendships sometimes involved a binding acceptance of constant companionship. Some girls were offended if you did not go everywhere together and spend every spare moment in each other's company. In those days, schools did not provide any kind of counselling service so there was no one to give advice or help us communicate and understand each other.

Vicky had probably been my most consistent friend during my three years at Queen Anne's. We would be best friends for a time and then drift apart probably from need of a change as much as anything else. Vicky nearly always seemed to be concerned about some aspect of her health. We used to make fun of her various troubles and the group called her a hypochondriac. Vicky left QAS to study for her A levels nearer home in Colchester and then went on to university in London. I met up with her later when she had an American boyfriend. They belonged to some Christian Society.

Di was a strong character and often lacked sensitivity. In the group, arguments usually started or revolved around Di and she always tried to come out on top. When I recorded our weights, Feri, Vicky and I were similar (just over 7 stone). Di was two stone heavier but not fat. Perhaps having a bigger build (and having two older brothers) caused her to be more competitive. My friendship with Di was full of emotional conflicts. She tended to go around telling the whole house about everyone's personal embarrassments. It was typical that she told everyone about me crying in an English lesson. Another time I fell out with Di because she was very competitive over exam results. I always struggled with my own sense of social inferiority. Most people want friends to laugh and have fun with. I was less popular because my timidity made me a serious companion. Social class is only a concept but it does affect the way we spend our time and our expectations. The other girls had the prospect of financial security once they left school. I always expect too much from people and then, of course, I am disappointed.

Diana left to do her A levels at Charterhouse one of the boys' boarding schools that had just started taking sixth form girls. She told us that the boys openly masturbated together in public. This was further evidence of boys' greater responsiveness. Diana had always been one of the brighter girls. I was surprised when she told me she hadn't chosen sciences or maths A levels. I could not understand why Di chose a traditional female career when she could have entered a higher-earning male profession. I assumed it was either family prejudice (that girls don't need to earn as much) or her own lack of ambition. In her last term, Di was friendly with Jenny. They met up in the holidays too, which offended me. I assumed that Diana wanted to be with her own social set. She and Jenny went on to do a degree in physiotherapy together in London.

Jenny was one of the older girls. She was easy to get along with and she made everyone laugh. Jenny was very popular and most of the girls wanted to be friends with her at some time or other. I assumed that Jenny was much too popular to want to bother with me. Equally I was reluctant to be her friend only to be passed over for someone else. I was proud and I didn't want to have to fight to keep someone's friendship. I was hurt if they ignored me or wanted to be with someone else. I was convinced that the other girls did not want to know me because I was too quiet or not trendy enough.

One term we were told that a new girl, Sarah, was joining our house. We were curious to meet her because she came from a state school. We expected her to be intimidated by our upper-class accents but she was very confident of herself. Sarah told us that she never did any work in her last school and so she happily admitted to being quite unintelligent. Sarah soon had us fascinated with her stories from the outside world, including boys and discos. In no time at all she was speaking in the upper-class accents of the school. Sarah became good friends with Jenny and they were often together. Louise was the other newcomer. It was clear from the beginning that she would not adjust so successfully. She had an American accent and kept to herself. She didn't invest any time in integrating with the rest of us. She seemed to spend most of her time on the phone to her boyfriend with no concern for cost. She was also a chain smoker. She flaunted the rules so blatantly that there was little the housemistress could do about it. She left after a couple of terms.

Around the age of fourteen or fifteen, one of the girls in my year accidently wet herself during a fit of giggles. This event sparked months of behaviour where many of the girls would deliberately urinate while fully dressed and dissolve into fits of laughter. I was not impressed. By the time we got to the sixth form, both Di and Vicky had gone. I had to make new friends. I was not part of the silly crowd so I had to choose between Amanda and Alison.

Amanda and I were not a natural match but we were put in a dorm together. Amanda told me she wanted to leave and I found out that Miss Challis did not think she would get her A levels. My other friend, Alison had talked about wanting to leave the school from the very first term. The reason became clear when the head mistress told Alison that she was not working hard enough. Alison was often teased by the other girls for being plump. She had a good sense of humour and mostly laughed along at the jokes. Alison's parents took me to Marlow regatta and I wore some dreadful skirt that I had made in sewing classes. Alison persuaded her brother Nick to take us to a dance. I was asked to dance by a man who turned out to be 24 years old. Men often seemed to think I was older than I was because of my serious demeanour. I allowed him to kiss me but noted in my diary that *'I didn't feel anything.'*

# A chance to think about morality and spirituality

Regardless of the penalties, there were always girls who smoked cigarettes. They went in small groups and smoked together behind the sports huts at the end of the field. I had no money for cigarettes but I wasn't remotely tempted. I enjoyed having a drink with my parents so I never felt the need to prove anything with either cigarettes or alcohol. As a small child, I had heard the government warnings about the health risks of smoking and I had often worried about my parents smoking. All the way through school, I tried to stop biting my nails but I never succeeded (until my forties). I decided that if I smoked, I would probably be a chain smoker like Jo. I knew how difficult it had been for her to give up smoking.

In February 1974, a girl called Ruffy was expelled for smoking. She was in the year above and I didn't know her. But she was a popular girl. On the day she left, the others girls kept playing the song 'When the carnival is over' over and over for hours on end on the record player in the common room. There were tears and a general atmosphere of mourning, which I thought a little melodramatic. Given that Ruffy had repeatedly broken the rules, I was not sympathetic. This might seem heartless given that smoking is addictive but there was an attitude that went with these girls. They were attention-seekers and used bravado to impress or intimidate.

Some of the girls at QAS went shop lifting for small items just for the dare. I was shocked by the dishonesty but also by the fact that they came from privileged families. Every year a funfair used to come to Caversham. In our senior years, everyone else sneaked out of the school at night to go it. If they had been caught, they would have risked expulsion, as this was a serious breach of the school's security. I wasn't interested because I don't enjoy fairground rides due to motion sickness. Another reason was that I have never enjoyed being in trouble. I had no good reason to break the rules.

When we were fourteen some girls in my year were caught drinking. I felt humiliated when we were all hauled into Leaks' room for a serious lecture about the evils of drinking. The alcohol involved was ginger beer with an alcoholic content of a quarter of a percent. I was drinking cider and wine with Jo during the holidays. So I was not tempted to waste my time breaking rules with ginger beer. Another time, some junior girls in my house got themselves drunk on a cocktail of spirits, cider and beer. Needless to say, they were caught. One girl was suspended and another was expelled.

Di invited me to stay with her one weekend. Her parents lived in a large house in a village near Guildford. We went swimming in the public pool at Guildford. Di dared me to jump off the high diving board, to attempt crawl and to open my eyes under water. I could do none of these things and she was irritated by my reluctance to try them. She had grown up in Malawi where the family lived an outdoor life so sport was very natural to her. I felt inadequate and her behaviour did not help me feel at ease. I was embarrassed and awkward all the time. Diana's father was the bursar of a boy's boarding school. I was impressed when he told me they read poetry together. I only read poetry at school and I could not imagine either of my parents taking an interest in such an intellectual pursuit.

Di's father asked about my family, which turned into what felt like an interrogation. Jo had asked us to say that Simon was our brother, instead of our half-brother, to try to cover up the fact that he lacked a father. But I hadn't given much thought to the answers I gave and it was fairly easy to spot the obvious error. My natural inclination is to be honest so I don't make a good liar. Diana's father quickly spotted the fact that Simon could not be Trevor's son. Rather than drop the topic, he wanted to know the date of my parent's divorce and how old Simon was. I felt that his insensitivity and persistency on such a personal matter was rude and inconsiderate. Perhaps he was just trying to expose the obvious contradiction in my story.

Simon's parentage was problematic because the reason for his father's absence could not be explained without embarrassment. Adults seem to assume that all children are a result of their parents being (at least initially) intent on a relationship for the longer term. Illegitimacy is not taboo anymore. There is no problem if you have parents who aren't married to each other. But there was never any intention that Simon's father would be part of the picture. It was awkward because there was no socially acceptable way to explain that Simon was the result of an affair Jo had with a married man.

Divorce was still relatively rare in the mid-seventies. So, I was used to the sympathetic response from adults on hearing that my parents were divorced. Still, I was surprised when a girl at school said she felt sorry for me. I explained to her that I could not remember my parents ever having been together. I had never known any different.

I was fond of my parents but I still wished sometimes that I had the respectable married parents of other girls. On the other hand, I was grateful that my parents were interesting people who rarely interfered in our lives. Middle class parents can be very controlling.

I often felt disadvantaged that there were so many aspects of my family to explain away. Trevor was unemployed but he had never had a career job with the social status that is expected of the middle classes. Anne's mental handicap was also an issue because no one ever talks about these conditions. Most people seem to be ignorant of the physical and mental disabilities some children are born with. In my French O level oral exam, I decided it would be easier to make something up. I got into difficulties but hoped these would be attributed to the language. Adults need to give more thought to the fact that not every child belongs to a model family. We all want to be accepted and conform to social norms. I thought it unfair that I had to explain my parents' choices. Perhaps, schools should not expect children to answer personal questions. Life is not neat and tidy. There are many domestic situations that are difficult to explain because of the taboo in society over unconventional families.

From the age of eight, Christianity was part of my school life. At the Sneep, we went to weekly church services. Queen Anne's had a proper chapel with pews and stain glass windows, which could accommodate the whole school as well as parents on public occasions. We went to chapel at the start of each day and we had to attend a Sunday service. The resident chaplain was a grey-haired man who administered at services and taught religious education at the school. Our religious education lessons involved understanding some of the moral lessons in the bible, which I appreciated learning about. I was interested in the intellectual ideas and moral challenges in some of the bible stories such as the Sermon on the Mount.

The school offered confirmation (entry into the Christian Church). As part of the preparation, I was called into an interview with Mr Smith. It was standard practice for him to write to the parents of girls asking to be confirmed and ask for parental support for their child's entry into the adult church. Trevor had evidently replied to the letter in an offhand manner. He was not a supporter of the Church. His whole adult life had involved a rejection of middle-class prudery and small-minded religious piety. I was disappointed that his lack of tact caused me so much distress. Mr Smith spent the whole interview telling me how unsuitable a candidate I was for confirmation given my parent's credentials. Mr Smith believed that Trevor's attitude would result in me losing faith in the future. I became tearful and upset, which caused me to feel intensely embarrassed afterwards. Once again, I felt let down by my parents.

My conclusion from this experience was that Mr Smith, despite being a priest, was not a compassionate person. He was a man in his late fifties. I was fourteen years old. I was shocked that he could be so relentless in verbally attacking my own character as well as my father's. He asked nothing about my family circumstances. His attitude was not only judgemental of my father's behaviour but he also implied that I would be exactly the same when I grew up. Given my experiences, I naturally dislike prudery. I have never had any respect for puritans who, in my opinion, lack experience of life. They assume that everyone has the same family background and experience that they have. So they naturally assume everyone has the same attitudes and draws the same conclusions about morality.

It was a good thing that Mr Smith knew nothing of my parents. Their sexual histories would no doubt have convinced him that they should be sentenced to hell and probably me too for being so stupid as to be their offspring. Luckily, he knew nothing of Simon's illegitimacy. But these issues are created by parents not by their children. I decided that being a good Christian was not about just going to church. I wanted to rely on my conscience to ensure that I always treated others with respect. Trevor wrote to me advising against inviting Jo to my confirmation. He thought that she might cause embarrassment somehow. However, Jo came and after having lunch in Reading, she returned home by public transport.

The chaplain commented on my attitude in religious education classes in my school reports. He noted that I often seemed puzzled. I wanted to understand the interpretation we were given of the moral lessons in the bible. Most people accept what they are told. Women especially do not offer opinions or directly challenge others. This is perhaps because many people become impatient, defensive or angry when their views are challenged. But I have never felt that it should be a crime to try to understand the world about me. I have always questioned inconsistencies or things I don't understand. I'm not deterred if other people try to evade questions. I assume that if they don't know the answer, they will admit the fact.

This zeal of mine to obtain logical explanations means that I am often oblivious to how uncomfortable people feel when they are put outside their comfort zone. I do not consciously set out to pressure people but I like to have answers that make sense. I need to be able to fit new facts into the understanding of life that I have accumulated from my experiences so far. I have always been interested in relationships and why people behave the way they do.

This character trait is a disadvantage in employment. Most successful people focus on promoting themselves. They are accepted because they agree with others in the group. You might wonder why I have never learned the basic survival skill of conforming. It just seems to be a fundamental part of who I am. Often, I don't need to say anything. My serious demeanour and privileged schooling speak for me. People assume that I must think of myself as socially superior, which I do not. They are intimidated by my directness and because I do not tolerate ignorant thinking.

In my research topic such characteristics are an asset because I have persisted where most people would have given up long ago. There are no personal rewards other than the satisfaction of finding explanations for my own experiences and other women's behaviours. I enjoy providing sex information and helping other couples understand the issues that may arise in sexual relationships. I have been persistent in trying to find answers that satisfy my intellectual curiosity. I dislike the sexual bravado that many women, who are willing to comment, use to intimidate others. People take advantage of sexual ignorance and embarrassment over sexual issues to promote their own ego. But it's essentially a bullying tactic.

## Academic competition and external examinations

The only aspect of school life where I felt I could earn some respect was on the academic side. At the Sneep, we rarely did revision except when we were preparing for the scholarship exams. So Feri and I came across revision for the first time. The others had done much more exam revision at their junior schools. I concluded that *"exams at QAS are rather silly. It is more of less, if you can memorise a lot in a little time then you do well."* Another difference was that at the Sneep we used to do our prep (homework) under supervised conditions so it wasn't possible to get help from others. I was shocked to see how many girls would compare notes with each other before completing their homework. I thought that sharing or copying other people's work and ideas was cheating. It perhaps explained why some struggled later because they had enhanced their marks up until that point by getting help.

At mealtimes, we senior girls sat at the end of the dining tables to serve and supervise the younger girls. I still hated making conversation even with juniors. Sometimes a member of staff joined us for lunch. One of the lower sixth had to accompany the visitor to lunch and act as their host during the meal. For me this was a nightmare scenario. I had to suffer the doubly embarrassing experience of hosting the school chaplain, Mr Smith. All I could think about was the humiliation of being in tears throughout my confirmation interview the previous year. Somehow, with considerable politeness on both sides, we got through the ordeal.

I still read a great deal. I especially liked novels with an historical theme. I enjoyed the peace and quiet of sitting in the school library. The library was at the end of the school assembly hall. It was on the first floor, which was accessed via two winding stone staircases in the towers at either side. The room was wood panelled and had wooden seats around the circumference below the lead-latticed windows. There were two turrets on each of the towers, which were so picturesque that a new art teacher spent weeks drawing them.

I often despaired of my ability to keep organised. *"Sometimes I depress myself. I have lost this book I have to write about by tomorrow. I don't know how I lost it!"* Someone had taken it back to the library so the next day I had to write my essay in an hour after reading only 80 out of 400 pages. My coping strategy was to try to get ahead of the game. I also used study as a means of keeping busy and not getting depressed. *"Felt very organised, working hard, practicing and domestics."* I seemed to find an endless list of things to be depressed about. Favourite topics were my shy personality, my looks and my lack of aptitude for sport or an academic subject. I also despaired of my friendships. My calls to Jo from the pay phones were my lifeline. I was often sick of school and of having to live in such close proximity with the other girls.

Anorexia was becoming a phenomenon among teenage girls and everyone had to be weighed regularly. In the Lower Fifth, I noted that I was the lightest of the senior girls including the year below. A number of the girls in the house developed anorexia. I was not close to any of the girls involved. But I concluded that it was further evidence of girls' nervous disposition (compared with boys) and women's universal lack of self-esteem. I always enjoyed eating and I didn't have a problem with my weight, so I never dieted for long.

I noted that in the first year the order of brains in Wilkins was Barley, Di, Feri and I and then the rest. I was always anxious before the exams that the magic might fade and I would suddenly stop getting good marks. When it came to it, I enjoyed the exams. French was my initial worry at senior school. When I started German in my second year, I found that even more challenging. However, my most hated subject throughout senior school was English. I lacked confidence in creative writing. Although I read a great deal, I was a lazy reader so I didn't have a good vocabulary. I skipped words I did not understand as well as tedious prose. I never knew what I should write about and dreaded putting pen to paper.

Miss Woolison, known as Woolly, was my English teacher. She was universally feared and hated. Some days passed off uneventfully but often she would pick on someone to humiliate. I was easily reduced to tears. I blamed my self-pity on the emotional upset of having a childhood deprived of a family home. We had to sign up to read parts in the play we were studying. It was tempting to sign up for only small parts but this would be spotted. So I had to judge how little I could get away with. I dreaded having to read for fear of bursting into tears. It angered me later to hear that Woolly admitted that her teaching style was based on intimidation. Di asked her parents to move her to another teacher. I was amazed that Di was bothered because she was always much tougher than me. I resented that I had no hope of the same parental support.

In the Easter holidays when I was fifteen, I had peritonitis and had to go into hospital to have my appendix removed. After twelve days in hospital I was allowed to go home. I had missed the beginning of term and my first public exams were about to start. I returned to school just two weeks before the start of my O level exams. I worried about not being well enough prepared for the exams: *"Got depressed about how little I have revised."* Another comment *"Got bored of revising"* appeared to indicate that some revision was being done. My ultimate coping strategy was based on my father's advice. He said we should not take exams too seriously. I was determined to leave QAS at the end of the year. Although I didn't want another year with the same people, Miss Challis advised me to stay on for the lower sixth. I chose my A level subjects: Maths, Physics and Chemistry on the basis of the teachers I liked.

Returning to school, we were in the Lower Sixth and called The Study. Barley was Head of House, Jenny was Vice Head and Ali was Head of games. I volunteered to be charity representative and then had a fit of panic and depression over the responsibility. We were all prefects and we enjoyed having the younger girls looking up to us. We had various duties, one of which was to supervise the younger year groups during their prep periods. It was a little nerve-wracking wondering whether they would test my authority and how I would react if they made fun of me. I did not want to get a reputation for being no fun but I also did not want to lose respect. Luckily all went well and I found I enjoyed being in authority.

In the sixth form we were studying for our A level exams and the amount of work increased substantially. We could use the reference library during free periods to do our prep. Whenever I got bored, I read books in the library on subjects that had nothing to do with my academic studies. I enjoyed reading books about astronomy and cosmology as well as those on mathematical puzzles. I also browsed through the Teach Yourself series on several topics, such as the Dutch and Russian languages. I had started teaching myself Italian as a hobby. When I was busy and everything was going well, I decided that school was not too bad. At other times, I became fed up with the routine. I hated sport and did not enjoy shopping so I was often at a loose end at weekends.

I was starting to wonder whether I would be continuing at Queen Anne's or whether I would be allowed to live with Jo for the second year of my A level course. I was concerned that if I stayed in a closeted all-female environment like a girls' boarding school, my development as a woman might be adversely affected. The only males I knew were my brother and my father. Granny had already talked about me leaving QAS. She must have been concerned about the effect of ever-increasing school fees on her capital. No doubt she also assumed we would spend our lives as mothers and not have much use for our education. Jo told me she had found a sixth-form college for me in Basingstoke. Trevor said to go ahead. Although I was excited about the idea of living at home with Jo, I was also concerned about such a dramatic change in my life.

I wrote off to find out about a university for the following year. I did not know what I wanted to do as a career. Every time I mentioned the subjects I was studying, everyone immediately thought I must be thinking of doing Medicine. I suppose that if I had been a boy, they might have suggested engineering but medicine was becoming a popular option for women. I knew that Grandpa had been a doctor and that Trevor had studied medicine. After a while I decided to go for medicine because it sounded respectable and was in line with my ideals of helping other people.

## School social dances and an introduction to men

After making a few hints, I did finally start piano lessons at the Sneep when I was eleven. I continued my lessons at Queen Anne's. My teacher was a grey-haired man with an old-fashioned manner. Mr King remarked on my quiet nature and he liked to hold my hand. His attentions were completely harmless but I was acutely embarrassed by this uninvited intimacy. At school, we used to refer to this male phenomenon as wandering hand trouble. It was apparent that women were not always in control of sexual situations with men. I was aware of how inappropriate his behaviour was but I lacked the courage and maturity to know how to deal with him. I was much too timid to tell him to keep his hands to himself. I was also afraid that if I reported him that I would still have to face him.

On my birthday, he gave me £2 and tried to kiss me on the mouth. Holding hands was one thing but I felt that mouth-to-mouth kissing with an elderly man was out of the question. I managed to avoid him on that occasion but I decided to give up my piano lessons. Jo was completely useless. When I mentioned the situation to her, she reacted with bravado, joking as if he was an eligible suitor. When I told Jenny and Barley about Mr King, they were shocked. At least they had some real-world reaction to such an awkward situation.

Alfred Kinsey talked about parents of young children who prosecute elderly men for gross misconduct. Kinsey's noted that men of this age are often impotent and so incapable of any sexual act. It's easy for a man to dismiss such behaviour as harmless. Even if nothing happens, women and children can feel extremely uncomfortable with men because of this lack of control. Men rarely have to deal with other men who are intent on physical gratification and they can usually defend themselves. Men control intimate situations because their own pleasure is the focus for the activity. Women tend to dislike any form of physical intimacy with a man they are not emotionally involved with (in love with or married to).

I have been conscious of my timidity throughout my life but especially as a young woman. Even as an adult, I am reluctant to talk on the phone. This timidity, that is typical of many women, is incompatible with having a sex drive. Men need a certain level of confidence in order to be capable of initiating sexual activity. That confidence comes in part from their sexual arousal, which gives men a justification for taking the sexual initiative. I was aware of no urge to initiate sexual activity of any kind. We talked about boys in social terms (not as sex objects). Rather than thinking about the possibility of sexual activity, we had a desire for platonic admiration.

It was clear from my reading that a woman's sexual role was to respond to the male initiative. Nevertheless erotic fiction seemed to imply that arousal and orgasm would mysteriously appear with a lover. I assumed that I would experience pleasure from sex but I never thought about how I would proactively obtain this pleasure. Masturbation provides a boy with an idea of how he might enjoy his own sexual arousal and orgasm through stimulating his penis with a lover. I was never consciously aroused during adolescence and so I was not tempted to investigate my genital responses.

Neither was it clear to me what I would do to obtain pleasure from a man's body. When I anticipated a sexual encounter, I was aware of my lack of control. I wondered what a man would do to my body. I had no similar urge to explore a man's body. I was not aroused by male nudity or by the prospect of sexual activity. My sense of adventure came later when I was in love. I had always enjoyed erotic stories that made a woman's role in pleasuring a man seem fun. But in reality, I felt no arousal. I made a conscious choice to behave proactively because I enjoyed being able to pleasure my partner.

I was not aware of any lesbian or masturbatory activity among any of the girls at school. Sex was never discussed. This is in strong contrast to the male experience. Teenage boys are often quite open about their use of masturbation. Boys also share their enjoyment of turn-ons, typically nude images. No woman ever discussed any aspect of sex with me. In fact, on one ever talked to me about erotic fiction, sexual fantasies, masturbation or sexual pleasure. A number of women refused to discuss any aspect of sex in such strong terms that it made me wary of ever mentioning the topic. It was this negativity that made me doubt portrayals of women's supposed responsiveness in the erotic literature. I have concluded that women do not discuss sexuality because they are not responsive.

Men are rarely required to account for their sexual activity. It's just called spreading their oats or playing the field. Women are not judged so positively for being sexually active. Society suggests that women can enjoy sex but then judges against them for being irresponsible. In the French novel 'Pierre et Jean' by Guy de Maupassant (1888), a woman has an affair. One of her sons is her husband's child but the other is the son of her lover. When sexual activity results in pregnancy, the child's life can be greatly affected by the woman's social situation. The over-riding issue is whether she has secured a father for her child. This is one of the reasons for the double standard relating to attitudes towards sexual freedom.

A dance was arranged at Leighton Park a local boy's boarding school. I danced with one boy but felt uncomfortable when he put his arm around me. I felt no natural inclination to be intimate with someone I had only just met. He was pleasant enough but I was too shy to know what to say. He asked me whether I would like to see his room but this was too adventurous for me. I dropped out after this first dance and decided not to embarrass myself further. I just stood on the edge and felt miserably inadequate as I watched the other girls tongue kissing within minutes of having met a boy.

My top concern was how to make conversation with a strange boy. The usual topics were pop music (about which I knew nothing), contemporary youth culture (even less) and the usual questions about family. The question that sent me into total panic was "where do you come from?" I never had an answer. I didn't have a home, let alone a hometown. I also felt socially disadvantaged because my father was unemployed and my mother was a housewife. I did not have a prestigious family background in a privileged social system.

Some of the other girls were living life more fully than I was. I was quite shocked by how openly they would boast of their adolescent sexual experiences. These experiences were used as proof of their greater worldliness and maturity as women. To me it all sounded crude and lacking in any romantic passion. When I read books about beautiful women, I wondered whether I was pretty. As my body developed and my breasts were starting to show, I found that all of a sudden, I was noticed by men. I would be just walking somewhere and a random man would make an admiring remark.

Some of these were good humoured and others were much less respectful. Men who made unpleasant comments seemed to think it was fun to insult women. Apparently, some men are aroused or amused by provoking a response from women even if it is only disgust or anger. On the whole I tried to focus on the positives and I enjoyed getting compliments. This feedback from men definitely influenced my subconscious. I contemplated how men might regard me. I became aware that they found me sexually attractive.

There was another dance arranged at Wellington College and it was on the day of my sixteenth birthday. There was much talk of 'sweet sixteen', which meant that a girl had not kissed a boy by that age. The idea was that this situation should be avoided at all costs. I remembered how I had felt at the last dance but I decided that I would have to force myself to overcome my shyness. My ambition level was set at the lowest level of kissing a boy. I had no desire to go any further than that. My religious education warned against sex outside marriage but also, I felt no need whatsoever to have sex.

Naturally, the occasion of a dance involved a great deal of preparation. We spent hours getting ready, bathing, dressing, doing our hair and make-up. When we arrived in the coach, it felt like a cattle market. A girl entered the room and a boy approached her for a dance. The dancing was no doubt just a front for many, a precursor to more adventurous petting activity. I accepted an invitation to dance with the first boy who approached me. Unfortunately, he was unattractive, both short and chubby. I was too embarrassed and immature to know how to change partners so I decided he would have to do. We danced together all evening. He was as inexperienced as me and said very little. I was hardly bursting with personality myself and I left all the initiative to him.

We kissed by having continuous mouth-to-mouth contact while slow dancing. The whole experience was very wet and not in the least arousing. Afterwards I felt ashamed of myself for feeling pressured into such intimate behaviour. I had no one to ask for guidance and had to draw my own conclusions. One girl who I had never considered either mature for her age or attractive, told me that she had let a boy put his hand down her dress and feel her breasts. I was shocked that she would let a stranger be so intimate.

Other encounters were not so innocent. At some of these dances a girl would fall pregnant, which shows the dangers of ignorance and desperation. These young people had never set eyes on each other before the dance night. These girls may have been hoping for sexual pleasure although I doubt they found it. There was certainly no time for romance. It was more likely that they were driven by curiosity and the ego of breaking social rules just for fun. I learned from the episode that I was only prepared to engage in intimacy with someone I found attractive and that I should only do what I was naturally motivated to do. I enjoyed light historical romance novels. This was how I decided I would choose a prospective lover. I would only have sex when I fell in love with a man who I admired.

# PART V: MY PARENTS

## Holidays with Jo and living the poor life

The centre of Kingsclere had the character of a village. Jo's house was on a small housing estate up the hill from the church. The rich people lived in large houses in the old part of the village around the Church. We attended church most Sundays. There was often a hunt for some small change for collection and if Jo couldn't find any, we didn't go. Even 2p was enough. As long as she could put something in the collection tray. I used to look at the rich people in church with their hats and expensive coats. It was another world.

Jo was very careful with her money. I only realised later that I got used to this economy. I quite enjoyed having to make do. As we had no permanent home, I never collected many possessions. This enjoyment of a simple lifestyle has stayed with me all my life. Jo's friend Maureen was at the opposite end of the spectrum. She was also on benefits but when she ran out of money, she just went along to the benefits office in tears and they paid for her furniture. Jo said that she would never have the nerve to do the same. She was proud and would have felt humiliated to beg for money. Jo always kept £100 in premium bonds as a safety net in case of emergencies.

As we were growing up, I had a much closer relationship with Jo and Trevor than Sarah had. I think they tried but my both parents struggled to draw Sarah out. I was older but, more importantly, I enjoyed listening to my parent's views and experiences. I invested effort in listening because I was interested in learning from them. I have always thought carefully about everything I experience. I could listen without feeling any pressure to change my own views. I do not believe everything I am told. I simply add new information to my current understanding of the world. I think about situations afterwards and judge my own behaviour as well as the behaviour of others. So I arrive at conversations, confident of my own view. Other people seem less willing to learn from others in this way.

In many ways, my relationship with both of my parents was closer than it might have been if they had been married, either to each other or to someone else. Jo and Trevor were essentially single, so there was no competition from another adult. Later I appreciated that my childhood had none of the marital discord that so many children experience. They occasionally moaned at us but we were never shouted at. Naturally, they never had to deal with any of the usual issues in raising children because we were in their care for such short periods. My parents were always approachable and they took me seriously. My parents talked about their own lives and interests. They rarely asked me about my views and experiences.

My parents were much more interesting than most other adults I met. I found the parents of the other girls at school very conventional by comparison. I think this lack of convention in my childhood probably explains why I have never felt comfortable with the middle classes. The most noticeable difference was that most people want to be well thought of by others. Jo was proud of being herself. She was happy to join in with children's activities with no regard for her age or for looking respectable. One day as Jo was riding down the hill on Sarah's bike, a girl asked her "Are you a lady?" Jo had no money but she took advantage of all the free opportunities she could. She joined the local public tennis club and in summer, we went down as a family to play tennis. She also joined the local amateur dramatics society and helped out at the school.

Simon attended the village state primary school and made friends easily. Since Jo was on benefits my brother was one of the poorest among his friends. However, within her limited means Jo provided the basics, toys and activities, similar to other children. Simon always had a good selection of toys for Christmas and birthday. He had a bicycle from a young age and spent much of his free time cycling around in the village with his friends. At fifteen I still did not have a bike of my own. Sarah had been given one for her birthday so Trevor arranged for my cousin Sue's old bike to be transported to Kingsclere. Now we could go out cycling together. One favourite outing was to go on the bikes down to the duck pond in the village.

During our stays, Jo struggled to cope with the extra load. She was often tired and I was disappointed when she went to bed early because I enjoyed our conversations. She used to threaten to send us back to London if we kept making work for her. But it wasn't a serious threat. I spent as much time as I could with her. For most weeks of the year, Simon and Jo lived alone. When we came home, Simon had to share everything. This never seemed to bother him as he was an easy-going boy. He played outdoors with his friends. We rarely played together as he was over six years younger than me. He did play with Sarah and even Anne when she visited.

I wasn't envious of Simon. We had separate lives. I never really thought that my life could be different to what it was. I enjoyed my education and accepted that it was a social privilege. But I was always unhappy about the separation from my parents. It's possible that I got on with them better though because of this separation. I idealised them in a way because I saw so little of them. I was a willing listener in part because I enjoyed having their attention. Neither Jo nor Trevor truly took responsibility for Sarah and me, in the sense of providing for us socially or financially. They never took us shopping for clothes or invited friends over for us to play with. We simply stayed with them in their homes during holidays.

Jo admitted that she lacked the patience to help with Simon's reading but in other ways she did her best for him. Jo was concerned about the effect on Simon of not having a man in the family. She seemed to think that this deprivation might cause him to grow up to be gay. One time she found him trying on her clothes. She went to the school to request a male teacher for Simon and she enrolled him in the boy scouts. She also encouraged his interest in football. Simon had priority TV viewing rights, which was sometimes irritating for us as we had no interest in football. Jo said: *"Simon was a very easy boy to please. All I had to do to keep him happy was to keep him supplied with a football and a bike. He was very good at going to church as well and joined the choir."*

Jo was still in touch with Simon's father Barney. She received the occasional postal order but there was no formal agreement for maintenance payments. One day Barney called and told Jo that he was leaving his wife. He asked if he and his four children could come and stay with us. Sarah and I were excited by the sensationalism of finally meeting Simon's father. We thought it was all a great adventure. Simon was probably too young to understand. Barney arrived in his car that evening with his children. I remember wondering what it would be like to have new brothers and sisters.

One night was fine but where was everyone was going to sleep if they lived with us? But morning came and Barney presumably came to his senses because they all left, never to be seen again.

As teenagers Sarah and I never had very much money so we were eager to babysit when we were asked. We were in popular demand from the mothers of Simon's school friends. Christopher's mother had an immaculate house with colour television and delicate ornaments. She always left a huge array of snacks in the kitchen: fruit, cake, biscuits and crisps. It was a treat for me just to watch television in colour. Sarah and I had school uniform but no one bought us casual clothes. So we sometimes bought cheap second-hand clothes from the jumble sales in the village. One summer I bought a pair of burgundy cords and cut the trousers off at the knee. I thought I was very trendy going around bare foot wearing these.

When I was fifteen, Jo took all of us (including Anne) to Swanage to stay in a caravan that was advertised in the newsagents in the village. On the way, the bus broke down so we missed the coach and had to take the train, which involved changing to a bus at the end. We finally arrived tired. Jo had brought provisions with her. She had frozen beef burgers: the thin and rubbery kind. We ate beef burgers every day for tea for the whole week. There were no complaints. We all liked them especially with ketchup. We spent the first day at the beach but it was cold and windy. Early on Jo ran out of money so I got some money out of my Post Office account and we all bought sweets. Then we lost the key to the caravan but luckily, we had left a window open so we just climbed in through the window. The following day Jo got another key. As soon as the weather improved, there was no wind and we all got sunburned.

Another summer we went camping in Cornwall. We rode our bikes nine miles to Basingstoke to catch the train. We got on the wrong train but eventually arrived at a campsite near St Agnes. Each day, we cycled to the beach. Often it was too cold to go swimming. The first warm day came after one week. Every evening Jo bought wine, which she and I drank while playing cards in the tent. One day we just sat in the tent while it rained. On our second last night, it rained so much that our tents filled up with water. We decamped to the launderette and waited for everything to dry in the tumble dryer.

An old couple kindly offered us a hot drink in their caravan while we waited. The following day it continued raining and we spent the day in the laundrette. We were glad to be leaving the next day.

In winter we caught the bus to Basingstoke and went swimming in the public indoor pool. In summer if it was hot, we took the bus into Newbury to go to the outdoor pool. As teenagers Sarah and I used to lie out in the garden on a sunny day to work on our tan as was the fashion at the time. Jo's friend Maureen had a car. Occasionally we went down to the south coast in her car to visit the beach for the day. Jo started driving lessons just after her thirty-sixth birthday. They cost £2.20 each in those days. Once she passed her test, she used to rent cheap cars from Rent-a-wreak and we visited the coast again. One weekend we went to Lee-on-Solent and were worried that the car would fall apart before we could get home.

When Simon was a boy, Jo was content to devote herself to providing him with a home and a happy childhood. Her social life revolved around the mothers of Simon's friends. She had no apparent interest in men. Given the readiness with which Jo talked about her experiences, she must have made an unusual companion even for an open-minded person. Every six months the chimney sweep used to come to clean the chimney. Jo enjoyed chatting with him and gradually came to know all his personal concerns. She told me that he always booked a double session because he found their chats useful marriage therapy. Despite the suspicious appearances, Jo always maintained that he just wanted someone to talk to.

We never talked about sex and my mother certainly never gave me any advice. At times, she appeared shockingly naïve. She told me once that she had only recently discovered that a French letter was a condom. I did not see my mother as someone to ask advice of. She had only been married for six years. Her marriage was the longest time she ever lived with a man but Trevor was often absent. All her affairs were short-term. She was not at all discriminating about who she had sex with. Jo seemed to lack confidence about standing up for herself with men. She was too timid to communicate openly. I assumed she liked being single because she could avoid the conflict involved in negotiating what she wanted.

My mother had been in mental hospital, she was uneducated and her sexual experience was based on one-night stands and affairs. Later when I met young women who had educated mothers, I was surprised that they had also never discussed sex. I wondered why educated women who had been married for decades would not be prepared to discuss their sexual experiences with a daughter. It seems that most women never share such intimate experiences with anyone honestly. In some ways, I had the advantage that my mother had no need to be loyal to a partner. She also lacked the supposed refinement of the more educated woman. Nevertheless, she was just as embarrassed about talking about sex as any other woman.

One day Jo told me about a book of explicitly erotic pictures she had borrowed from a friend. But when I asked to see the book, she wouldn't show it to me. I don't know why she told me about it. Perhaps she was showing off. I find it amazing that people engage in sexual activity that they are embarrassed to acknowledge. Jo was happy to be seen topless but she thought it was crude not to wear knickers. I never understood why. Women seem to think that men's response to their anatomy makes these body parts disgusting in some way. Later I concluded that women do not understand what responsiveness involves. Women are offended by male arousal (that depends on seeing nudity) because they evidently don't understand that arousal occurs as a response to erotic stimuli.

## Jo's pride and resentment over our education

On the Saturday before my thirteenth birthday I spent the day at Jo's house. I noted in my diary that it was closest I had ever been to spending a birthday (that I could remember) with my mother. I had my most intimate and interesting conversations with her. So I was disappointed if time passed without the opportunity for us to have a deep and meaningful chat. For me it was always important to feel close to someone by talking about the things that mattered to me, mostly relationships and family. On 24th August 1974, I wrote *"Horrible leaving here! I LOVE MUMMY."* Jo was the person I was closest to. Returning to school was now more difficult.

I enjoyed feeling that Jo appreciated my help and my companionship. I helped her in the kitchen while she prepared meals and we did the dishes together. We took turns to wash or dry up. There was a dartboard on the wall and she and I would often play while a meal was cooking. I would help with simple tasks such as preparing the custard or mashing the potatoes. Sarah was rarely included in this domestic routine or our conversations. For her, washing up or helping with the cooking seemed to be just a chore. Jo and I also walked down the hill to the village to do the shopping or the laundry in the launderette. When Jo started working at the chicken farm, I was pleased to stand in as the carer for the family.

For me, it was always very easy to adjust to life in Kingsclere when we returned from school. The moment I walked in through the door, it was as if I had never left. Sarah did not have the same experience. My impression was that she was just settling back into our life with Jo when it was time to leave again. On one occasion when it was time for us to go back to school, Jo said that she would work on her allotment to forget how she was going to miss us.

Over the years, the most rewarding time that I spent with Jo was increasingly combined with our evening drinking. As I reached teenage years, Jo started treating herself to a trip to the off-licence on a Saturday night. She bought a cheap bottle of wine and a large bottle of fizzy drink for the others as well as one small packet of crisps each. Later this ritual was extended to Wednesday nights as well. In the winter months, we had late night snacks of baked potatoes, corn on the cob or cheese on toast. Regularly through my teenage years I wrote in my diary that I had drunk too much the night before. The next day I often dosed until midday. I used to make and break countless resolutions to stop drinking too much.

For many years, Jo made her own wine so that she had a cheap supply of alcohol. She used natural ingredients such as elderflowers, elderberries or dandelions from the countryside so the most expensive ingredient was the sugar. We collected sloes and Jo told us how poor people used to make sloe gin years ago. She intended building up a collection of wines that she could keep for a few years. Some of her wines could be quite drinkable. But soon she started drinking them while they were still fermenting.

Although I felt ill afterwards, at the time I was perfectly lucid and could converse sensibly. I enjoyed the opportunity to talk about my mother's life in a way we rarely did during the day. For the most part, she talked and I listened. She told me of her experiences growing up and her relatives. She talked in very general terms of her marriage, the Hares and Trevor's various failings. She rarely asked me in turn anything about my life at school, my concerns or my friendships. While I was a passive listener, the relationship worked well. Things changed later when I was more interactive.

In her late thirties, Jo had an unflattering perm which gave her an old-fashioned look. As a consequence of her deprived childhood, Jo had lost all her teeth by the age of thirty-six. She kept her dentures in a glass on the bathroom windowsill sterilizing overnight. I remember her often complaining of painful mouth ulcers caused by ill-fitting false teeth. In keeping with her class and background, Jo drank cups of tea (later also instant coffee when she had more money) all day long. It was either a cigarette or a cup of tea that she had in her hand. The tea was made with four teaspoons of sugar, despite the cost. It never seemed to occur to her to give it up.

Jo had been a chain smoker all her adult life. In February 1974, she tried for the third time to give up smoking. This time she was determined that if she gave up, she would never smoke again. Whenever Jo felt her will power weakening, she went to see her friend Maureen. Each time Maureen managed to talk Jo out of going to the shop to buy cigarettes. Smoking had helped Jo keep slim. Now she found that she needed to diet each summer. Her diets never lasted for long but she was keen to keep her figure.

At one time, Jo looked into buying a bed and breakfast business in Bournemouth. We went down to Bournemouth to have a look at a property but Jo concluded that it would not be possible. Jo told me that she wanted Trevor to be a silent partner in a business but she did not think he would do it. She needed about seven thousand pounds more than the house was worth. But the banks wanted fifteen thousand back, so she gave up the idea. Another time Jo wrote to say she was planning to buy a fish and chip business. I was impressed with all these ideas but they seemed quite incongruous compared with the social context of middle-class parents at school.

As I reached my teens, I was becoming increasingly conscious of the social gap between my school friends and my home life. We had never had expensive clothes or toys, horse riding lessons or a busy social life. We were used to being without material possessions or privileged opportunities. I also became aware of the intellectual ground that some of the other girls covered in the holidays. I felt disadvantaged when they returned to school having been exposed to their educated parents' political or philosophical debates. I returned certainly refreshed but my only exposure to the outside world was Simon's soccer on the television and Trevor's largely uninformed rants about the demise of the Great British Empire.

I was slow to invite my school friends to Kingsclere. I looked forward to the private time that Jo and I spent together on these weekends. I was also self-conscious of the extreme social contrast. Feri and I had met at the age of eight and she first saw how we lived at home when we were fifteen. Although Feri had never entertained me at her house, I felt it was easier for her to amuse friends because she had the backdrop of an educated family and a large house. When I eventually invited Feri to Kingsclere, I felt obliged to forewarn her that Jo's house was different to the homes of the girls at school. Feri said that she was not shocked at all. She made some positive comments. Jo's house was small but it was clean. The social implications for us growing up were probably missed on teenagers.

Although I felt at ease with Jo, her life and her views, as we grew up it became evident that she harboured some resentments over the opportunities we had. I have often found that people feel inferior when faced with someone who is more educated. It's difficult to appreciate how it feels when you have the confidence of an education. I have always been a serious person and this seems to upset some people. Many people prefer to fool around rather than discuss serious topics. Jo had only learned to read and write. I was thinking of going to university. The gap was potentially huge. One day she told me that she thought Sarah and I might never marry because we were too educated. She also told me that she thought I might never have children because I had not grown up in a family.

I covered up my feelings because of pride but I was very hurt by these remarks. I felt that such negative comments indicated that Jo didn't identify with me on a personal level. They made me feel rejected. Jo also commented on my lack of maturity. Where she expected my maturity to come from, I don't know. Parents seem to expect children to grow up through experiences outside the home rather than preparing them in advance for what they might meet. I played with my soft toys until I went to senior school at the age of twelve. I also played imaginative games in the countryside well into my mid-teens. Neither of our parents made any effort to encourage us to have a social life outside school or introduce us to any boys.

One half term, we went to London and, rather bizarrely, Jo came to stay. This was the first time that I had seen my parents together. My impression was that they were curious to see each other. Trevor gave Simon special attention and I felt a little jealous. Jo took us back to Kingsclere by train. She hadn't bought a ticket for Simon so I had to go to the toilet when the conductor came. The visit helped bring Jo back to earth. During the early years at Kingsclere, Jo still had romantic illusions about Trevor. But after this visit, she decided she didn't want him getting too close to Simon. Trevor wrote to Simon afterwards but the correspondence soon died out.

After this Jo started thinking about having relationships with other men. Once a week she dressed up to go to a singles club with Maureen. Jo had a series of boyfriends who came and went. We rarely liked any of them. None of them showed any interest in us. They never stayed overnight. They only came for a few hours. They used to have a meal and then have sex. I did not like to think of Jo having sex with these men. If she went to bed with a man in the middle of the day, I went up to the playing field to get away from the house. I did not want Jo to marry because I knew that our relationship would change. I enjoyed feeling close to Jo when we talked. When a man was around, there was no chance to talk.

Jo's younger brother Tom suddenly re-entered her life in February 1975. They had not seen each other for nine years because his first wife had been jealous of the close relationship between brother and sister. Now that Tommy had separated from his wife, he resumed their friendship. Each was single and looking for a new partner, so their social lives overlapped for a time. Tommy had a daughter, my cousin Helen, who was a year younger than I was. Helen went to state school and already had a serious boyfriend by the time she was fifteen. One evening Tommy arrived with Helen to take Jo out and I was mortified to be left at home with the children. Jo thought Helen was more mature than I was even though I was a year older.

Sandra, the daughter of Jo's old friend Jenny, was the same age as me. Sandra went to the local state school and was a regular smoker. She had a sexual relationship with her twenty-year-old boyfriend. Jo evidently believed that these behaviours, that are associated with being adult, indicate a true maturity. I have concluded that young women act the way they do out of ignorance and due to a lack of choices in their lives. Engaging in intercourse is easy for a woman. She doesn't need to be aroused. Having intercourse may result in a girl becoming pregnant but it does not indicate that she has intellectual maturity (questioning her place in the world), personal maturity (being able to support herself financially) or sexual maturity (being curious about her own responsiveness). My own immaturity was probably due to my intelligence and imagination. Ironically both of these character traits led to me having a high-earning career and the erotic fantasies that make orgasm possible.

## Learning about my father and my parent's divorce

Now that I was a teenager, Jo said rather mysteriously that she wanted me to discover by myself why she had divorced Trevor. Slowly I became more certain that I might know the reason but I was nervous of broaching the topic. I had started to question my father's sexuality. Apart from his 6-year marriage to my mother, he had always been a bachelor. I had no direct proof and it seemed a terrible thing to accuse my father of. My father was not effeminate in his mannerisms. I had no one to discuss my suspicions with.

By the time I was fourteen, Trevor was living in London and sharing his flat with a young Scot, called Alan, who was twenty years his junior. It was this long-term relationship with another man that helped me conclude that he was gay. There could hardly be any other explanation for two men sharing a bedroom. One evening over a bottle of wine, Jo and I had a long talk about Trevor. I thought it unfair of Jo to leave me the responsibility for opening the discussion of such an embarrassing subject. On the other hand, she was the only adult who ever discussed my father's sexuality with me.

Although I felt sorry for myself, I could see that my father's sexuality was personal to him. It had affected his life much more than mine. I realised that as a young man he must have been very confused. He lived in a world that said men should be attracted to women. There were references to homosexuality in literature but in everyday life, no one would have talked about it. Like so many young people in his position, there was no one for him to talk to. Neither were there any explanations for why fate should have decided to make him different. Homosexuality was legalised in the UK in 1967, when my father was 47 years old. In the 1990s his lawyer in the North of England commented to me that Trevor was the first man he had ever seen openly acknowledge his relationship with another man. There is a big difference in attitudes towards alternative lifestyles between big cities and provincial towns. Trevor was nevertheless ahead of many others in not hiding his sexuality.

When I was sixteen Jo told me that Trevor was not the biological father of any of us. I was sceptical because it seemed very convenient for her to suggest this now. While it had suited her, she had been happy to have Trevor named as our father. It seemed to me that she was intent on hurting someone, either us or him. But I accepted that it was unlikely that a gay man would ever father a child. Jo provided some vague details of the men she thought might have been our fathers. I concluded that I should keep an open mind. After all Simon's difficulties with illegitimacy, it was ironic that he was the only one of us who knew actually knew who his father was. This highlights the contradiction in our society, which gives preference to marriage certificates rather than true biological facts. I resolved that when I had sex, I would be discerning enough to be able to tell any resulting offspring who their father was.

George Caldwell wrote: *"Derry Baird told the story of how he and your father always slept together in the same bed at The Tower when he stayed. It was some time after the War, he said, when Granny introduced the subject and said 'Derry. I think it is time and you are old enough to have your own room, now!' Both must have been in their mid to late twenties!"*

Naturally my grandparents never referred to their son's homosexuality. They may well have blamed Jo for making the issue centre stage during the divorce proceedings. Jo told me that she had been unaware of Trevor's sexuality before they married. Jo was experienced with heterosexual men. Maybe she couldn't accept that not all men like women. As they settled into married life my father took no trouble to hide his relationships, which he continued to have with other men. Jo wrote: *"He continually brought men back at the weekend, sometimes famous people but always men."*

In April 1965 Jo listed for her solicitor the thirty-two 'points of cruelty' that supported her petition for a divorce. She claimed that Trevor had put pressure on her to have sex with complete strangers, men as well as women. He also brought strangers home to have sex with overnight. Once he brought a man to bed and had sex with him while Jo was in the bed. He also set aside rooms in the Bayswater house for his homosexual activities. It's possible that Trevor made the mistake of thinking that women of the lower social classes are more sexual than educated women. Even promiscuous women, like my mother, can be incredibly prudish. Women lack the responsiveness that makes erotic scenarios attractive to men.

Jo said: *"He was not able to have sex with a woman. We would sleep together but he was not able to get an erection. I thought nothing of this and was probably pleased because I was not keen myself."* Later she contradicted this picture of a sexless marriage by saying: *"I do not remember much about my sex life with Trevor. I do know that to make it possible he had to imagine he was with a man every time we had sex."* Jo never talked to me about anything remotely intimate or sexual. I assumed that this was due to embarrassment as it usually is with women. So I am sure she never discussed the intimate aspects of her marriage with anyone. Most people would not have believed her. So, a facade of a normal marriage and family life was maintained for the benefit of others.

Some of Jo's criticism of Trevor I can identify with, especially his problem with money and the effects of parental control. I also knew that he had a selfish side to his nature that ultimately destroyed his intimate relationships. I decided to focus on my own experience.

Trevor was a loving parent. He was proud of my achievements and in his own way he did his best to care for me. I found it difficult to be too critical of my parents because I loved them. I have taken the view that there's a good and a bad side to everyone. George Caldwell said: *"Your Dad was a bit complex: sometimes selfish and more often generous. I think you have given him a fair trial."*

Jo always referred to homosexuals as queers. I think the word summed up what she saw as their deviant sexuality. She advised me not to discuss homosexuality at school. With the topic now out in the open at home, Jo started referring to homosexuals all the time. She always told us which film stars were gay and it seemed to me that most of them were. I started to wonder if there were any men who found women attractive at all. Later I wondered if my father being gay might affect my own sexuality. I decided it was unlikely. I could see that other women struggle to understand male sex drive as much as I did because women have no comparable experience.

When I had my first sexual relationship, I initially thought my lack of response might be due to a lack of exposure to men. But I have not found other women to be any more knowledgeable or more comfortable with sex than I am. In fact, the reverse is often true. Gay men treat women like people. Other women are repulsed by the way their heterosexual male relatives treat them. They are made to feel like pieces of sexual meat. Naturally having a gay father made me sensitive to the jokes and innuendo that surround homosexuality. There is a misconception that all gay men are effeminate. The truth is that most gay men look and behave much the same as straight men. The gay culture is diverse but it is a world of men and my impression was that it is masculine and macho.

The only details I have of my father's life, came from his cousin George Caldwell. Trevor never revealed personal insights. Shortly before he died, Trevor told me that in many instances he was ashamed of what he had done. He believed that being sent to a boys' boarding school made it more difficult for him to grow up heterosexual. He suggested men just need a push to put them on the correct heterosexual path. Personally, I have concluded that orientation is innate. We are born that way. It's not an abnormality. It's just part of our personality. It is certainly not a conscious choice.

# Holidays with Trevor and living the rich life

As we reached teenage years, Sarah and I found the time we spent with Jo was much more enjoyable than the time we spent in London. At Kingsclere Jo had established a home. We spent time together as a family doing simple things like watching television together or playing outdoors. We could ride our bikes, go for a walk or go to the shops. Trevor was resentful of our obvious preference to be with Jo. He must have talked about it because Sarah and I were often invited to go up to The Grove for Christmas. It was awkward to turn-down these offers and naturally this job fell to me. We were visitors in these other houses. The house at Kingsclere felt like a home to us even though we were seldom there.

It was becoming increasingly difficult for Trevor to spend time with us. He did not know what to say and doing things always involved spending money. At least a couple of times each holiday Trevor took us to the cinema or the theatre. We did not have our own room and slept on the sofa or floor in the lounge or in the spare room if no one else was staying. For the most part, we only spent time with Trevor at mealtimes. He had his friends and errands to run but these did not include us. Even in the evening, he used to watch television in his own bedroom. During the day, my father left us to amuse ourselves. I spent the empty hours reading, which left Sarah at a loose end. Trevor often commented that it was not healthy for me to read all day long but there was nothing else to do.

When I was fourteen, Trevor took me to Paris for half term. We stayed with people he knew and I was impressed with his ability to communicate. He knew little French but he made the most of facial expression and hand gestures. His efforts helped me appreciate that learning a language is more about a motivation to communicate than having any technical knowledge. Another time, Sarah and I went to Paris with Trevor and Barbara. We saw all the sights together. Next, we flew to Zurich where Uncle Alastair joined us. The plan was to drive a car back to England for Trevor's friend Jack. Trevor and Alastair took turns to drive back across France while Sarah and I sat in the back, playing games with Barbara.

For another half-term week Trevor took us to Switzerland and we stayed in a flat in Berne belonging to Trevor's friend Jack. We travelled around Lake Thun visiting the pretty towns of Spiez and Interlaken. Then we took the train up to the glacier on the Jungfrau mountain. Another time Feri, Sarah and I travelled alone to Zurich. Trevor had arranged for us to stay on a farm. Our hosts were an old German-speaking Swiss couple. There was nothing to do so we spent most of the day sitting around reading. We also played cards and picked cherries for hours, eating all the cherries we picked. Their ten-year-old daughter, Marianne, used to hang around hoping that we would play with her. Our days were divided by mealtimes, which were difficult as our German was very basic. We also did a couple of sightseeing trips: once to Thun and Oberhofen where we swam in the lake and another time to Bern. On August 1st, we went to see the fireworks for Swiss Independence Day.

In the summer months, Trevor took us abroad as a way of spending time with us. He did not like to spend money on others. He bought us small presents at Christmas and on birthdays. I was too proud to ask him for money but when I was fourteen, I summoned up the courage to ask Trevor for an allowance. The other girls at school had a regular allowance from their parents for clothes, sweets and toiletries. Trevor reluctantly agreed to send me money on an occasional basis. Once I was a teenager, Trevor let us travel around London by tube. I was proud that I could travel on my own at thirteen years of age. Once Trevor asked me to take Sarah to John Lewis to choose her school uniform and he arrived later to pay.

In the lower sixth, Feri came to stay with us in London. I asked Trevor if we could go to Trafalgar Square by tube. Initially he refused to let us go until his friend commented that we were no longer children. My father made friends easily. His friends liked him because, in his most extrovert moods, he was fun to be with. He was an interesting conversationalist and he could often see the amusing side of any situation. In turn he craved companionship. Trevor did not like to be alone. In his darker moods, he had bouts of depression and self-pity. Mostly we had a close relationship.

When we went home for the summer holidays of 1974, Trevor had moved from Gloucester Road to Earlscourt Square. He had bought a basement flat with a tiny galley kitchen, a lounge and two bedrooms. I noted that as Trevor was spending his capital, he was obliged to move further away from the centre of London and into smaller properties. Trevor paid to have the flat renovated with new decoration and carpeting. He had a brand-new galley kitchen fitted, with all the modern down-lighting. Trevor had expensive tastes but no practical skills. He spent extravagantly on renovating properties but without any idea of how to recoup the cost. I noted in my diary how different it was for him compared to Jo because he never gave a thought to cost. The flat had a long thin layout based on a corridor with rooms on one side. Half-way down, the corridor widened and there was space for a dining table where we ate meals together.

In Earls Court, Trevor started living with a much younger man. Alan was slim, attractive and usually dressed in smart casuals. Alan was from Scotland but he had lived in the South for many years. He still had a slight accent and was evidently educated. Alan had grown up in a fairly typical family. He didn't have any inherited capital and he was unemployed. So Trevor felt justified in expecting Alan to keep house to some extent. There were parallels with his marriage to Jo. I always got on well with my father until teenage years. I think the change had more to do with his relationship with Alan than with my adolescence. Of course, they had to manage their relationship with ups and downs during our holiday visits.

We ate together at lunch and dinner, which could be excruciating. Conversation was often awkward. The heavy atmosphere made me feel uncomfortable. I tried to make conversation as best I could, in an attempt to improve the atmosphere. It was accepted that Sarah never said anything. Many times, I had to accept defeat. I told myself that the responsibility to make conversation was not solely mine. When Trevor had spent hours preparing a meal, we had to eulogise about the food otherwise he got irritable. I started each holiday vowing not to get depressed but found his moodiness difficult to deal with. I think it's possible that he struggled with aging because he often talked about dying. Perhaps Alan's youth and the natural gradual decline in his own ease of arousal depressed him.

As we were growing up Trevor started expecting us to help around the house. His demands, fuelled by comments from his friends who did not have children of their own, do not seem unreasonable to me now. However, as a teenager, I was used to my mother doing the housework. When I met up with my father's friend Jack years later, I was quite taken aback when he commented on how spoilt we were as teenagers. We were certainly not spoilt in the sense of being indulged. I decided that what he noticed was more likely my wilful and independent nature as well as the universal teenage sloth.

## A man's idea of a teenage sex education

Trevor had approved of hugging and physical contact when we were children. Now he commented that I was sloppy. I think he meant affectionate but perhaps overly so. I understood that he felt that close physical contact was inappropriate now that I was becoming a young woman. He suggested that I was getting too big to sit on his lap. I took the hint and accepted that physical contacts between adults have a different significance. Thereafter, it was only on meeting and parting that I would give him an affectionate hug.

One of George's friends, Chris, was a doctor out in Malaysia but he spent a year in London. He rented a room from Trevor while he was still living in the house at Gloucester Road. A few days before I started at Queen Anne's, I noticed Chris larking about like a schoolboy with Trevor. The explanation for all the whispering became clear when Trevor approached me and said he had to talk to me about sex. Parents had been asked by the school to ensure their daughters were informed of the 'facts of life'. I thought their behaviour a little juvenile especially given Chris' medical training.

To save Trevor any unnecessary embarrassment I explained that I was already aware of the basics. Once started he evidently felt the need to say something so he explained the phenomenon of the male erection. This was news to me and I remember being pleased to add this fact to my store of sexual knowledge. Sex education is so often confined to the biological and anatomical facts that people feel more able to explain. The emotional and social issues surrounding sex are typically omitted. There was no sex education at Queen Anne's. I remember only one lesson on human biology when the female teacher produced a picture of a naked man that was passed around the class amid much giggling. I can't remember a word of what she said. I'm sure it was low on any factual detail.

Trevor grew up in a world of authoritarian women. The women were kept in their place, as wives and mothers, but they were strong and educated characters. Such women did not display any sign of their sexuality. The morals of the time were that only lower-class women displayed themselves provocatively and were referred to as tarts. Women of breeding were above such crude behaviour. It is a common misconception that upbringing or culture affect women's attitude towards eroticism. Men fail to appreciate that it is male responsiveness that makes them respond positively to eroticism (because they are aroused by it). A woman lacks the responsiveness that makes genital activity so attractive to men. Of course, as a gay man, Trevor had no experience of a woman's sexuality. He had based his life around sex, both inside and outside relationships, and he wanted his daughter to grow up to be a modern sexual woman.

One way in which Trevor attempted to encourage my interest in sex was to send me books that he had read. Many of these had a sexual theme. He enjoyed historical novels where the daughters of the aristocracy and royalty were often married according to the wishes of the family to men they disliked. All the sexual advantage was in favour of the men concerned who either forced themselves on their wives or looked for sexual gratification elsewhere. Men were in control and women were pursued. The reality of what this would be like for a woman presumably never struck my father.

Trevor liked light historical novels and short stories. One author we both enjoyed was Somerset Maugham. I was particularly interested in his observations on human nature. Maugham helped me appreciate men's sexual needs and women's disgust at them. Men had mistresses because their wives were sexually unwilling. 'Rain' was a story that I did not understand at all when I first read it at the age of 14. An old missionary couple arrive on a tropical island during the monsoon season (hence the title). They are shocked to find staying in the same hotel a seasoned prostitute of questionable class entertaining a series of male customers in raucous merriment. After spending some time with the prostitute, the missionary converts her to a more subdued Christian outlook.

Then suddenly the missionary commits suicide and the prostitute returns to her old occupation. But her attitude is openly derisive and bitter towards the prudish widow. There is no explanation of what has happened and as a teenager I could not read between the lines. Of course, the missionary was tempted into carnal relations with the prostitute despite all his claimed disgust at her occupation. She loses respect for him, presumably concluding that all men are alike. Many of these adult stories are never explained explicitly. The same is true of movies, which depict scenarios we know to be true but that are never acknowledged in explicit terms by anyone.

Catherine Cookson wrote light historical stories that focused on women's lives. She was always very explicit about the differences between the sexes. For me it was useful to have men's sexual urges so honestly acknowledged. It was also useful to have women's dislike of all things sexual out in the open. It's ironic that she wrote about the past. We have gone backwards since the sexual revolution. Today erotic fiction dominates and bravado makes it difficult for anyone to compare notes. Despite all the talk of sexual freedom, a loyal marriage is still a goal for most heterosexuals.

Although both of my parents were very open about being sexually active during my teens, neither of them ever referred to sex in any way. They certainly did not discuss their own activities and their motivations. I suspect that they were ashamed of what they did, knowing that society disapproves of irresponsible promiscuity. Although neither of them referred to sexual pleasure, it was clear to me that my father's motivations were quite different to my mother's. My mother often had sex when she was inebriated. She was lonely and looking for companionship. My father focused on physical gratification. As a man, he was able to travel the world and have sex with many different partners with no intention of ever having a relationship. My mother had indicated that she was embarrassed or disgusted by eroticism. My father obviously enjoyed sexual activity and eroticism in a way that I could identify with from my masturbatory activity. In different ways, both of them were just looking for someone to love them, as we all do ultimately.

Trevor had no sexual experience with women, apart from his marriage. So naturally he thought it must be possible for a woman to enjoy sex as much as a man. The fact that prostitutes were benefiting financially from their work clearly never occurred to him as significant. Much as it never occurred to me as a young woman reading erotic fiction. I have often wondered why fathers do not encourage their daughters to see sex as a positive aspect of their lives. I assume that married men leave any discussion of sexuality to their wives. Perhaps men, recognising that their wives are not interested in eroticism, assume that their daughters also won't be.

In August 1975, I set off for Frankfurt in Germany to stay with a family for a month. My father had met the couple on a nudist beach in Yugoslavia and on hearing that I was learning German, they had invited me to stay with them at their home in a small village near Darmstadt. Both parents were charming, educated and spoke perfect English. The father was a dentist. The family took me to Heidelberg to see the castle and the fireworks. I was much too self-conscious to learn any German. They introduced me to some German girls but I was intimated by kids of my own age. I was not interested in the pop music and boys (dressing-up or make-up) that other girls were so infatuated with. I felt so inadequate and was conscious that I was hardly a confident and well-balanced teenager.

My hosts were obviously liberal in their views. They had given me the guest bed-sitting room in the basement. There were shelves full of English language light adult-themed novels. As I had nothing else to do during my stay, I spent most of the time reading alone in my room. Many of these stories portrayed women as if they enjoyed sex for their own pleasure. Erotic fiction, admittedly often written by a male author, implied that women experienced the same kind of arousal and orgasm from intercourse that men do. An historical novel set in the days of slavery described the activities in erotic terms even though coloured women were the unwilling partners of white slave owners. The novels were easy to read and more explicit than the ones my father sent me. I enjoyed the sexual adventures.

For the first time, I contemplated how men might react towards me as I was becoming a woman. This was helped by living in a house with men who were not related to me for the first time. I only saw the father and the 16-year-old son at mealtimes. So I didn't know much about them. Nevertheless, they represented male figures who could substitute for men I wanted to be noticed by. During my stay in Germany I had my first period. I was fourteen years old and I was relieved that I was a woman at last. I noted with interest that I did not feel any different to before. There was a big gap until the second one and it was almost a year before they became regular.

I had other sources of erotic literature through girls at school who brought books from home and passed them around. I found these stories about the exploits of prostitutes or promiscuous women were enjoyable stories as well as an interesting source of sex information. They fuelled my anticipation of sex with a real man. Erotic fiction gave me the expectation that intercourse would be amazing but I had no sense of needing to make anything happen in real life. The social consequences were always uppermost in my mind. I was concerned foremost with the morality and social proprietary of sexual activity. My contemplation was romantic rather than erotic. I imagined kissing and a coupling of bodies. But I had little interest in what would be happening between my legs.

While I was in Germany Sarah had gone to stay with a friend in Portugal. I was envious that Sarah had friends who invited her to go abroad with them. However, she told me afterwards that she had not enjoyed her stay because the father had a drinking problem. I realised that other children did not always have ideal family lives despite their parents being married. I felt very grateful that my parents were not argumentative and never got aggressive. We have the impression that ideal families exist because no one talks about the challenges, the arguments and the bad behaviour. Our shame causes us to hide these problems, which in part causes the social taboo because everyone thinks they are alone in their experiences.

## Trevor, the silver spoon and his parents' money

Jo was fond of saying that Trevor was born with a silver spoon in his mouth. She told me about when they were married. Trevor used to spend money recklessly but Granny always paid his debts. He would furnish the whole house and then change everything on a whim. When Trevor bought the mews house in Bayswater, he raised a bridging loan from the bank. Unfortunately, the house in Lightwater had various structural problems and so it didn't sell. In the end, the property was sold as building land. This much lower value did not cover the bridging loan and the cost of the new house.

Jo never knew how much he owed but she knew it must have been a substantial sum. Jo wrote: *"as usual there was nothing to worry about because Mrs Hare came and paid it all as she always did."* When Granny rang to say that she was coming to sort it out, Jo asked her why she did not leave it to Trevor. Mrs Hare replied that he would end up in prison. Jo retorted that if she did that then at least Trevor might learn something. Later Granny explained to Barbara that they believed in leaving money to their children equally in a will, but during their lifetime they gave money to their children according to need. Taking into account the combined costs of Barbara's operations and Trevor's lifestyle and divorce, the Hares certainly did spend a great deal of money on their children.

Trevor had two main problems with money. In the first place, he had no motivation to earn any money. His friend, Jack, owned an English language school in Holborn. For a time, Trevor was employed there to do some light work and basic errands. He even took a course to become an English teacher but it came to nothing. As someone who lacked the ability to generate income, Trevor's financial management revolved around preserving what he had. Trevor was impressed with Jack's knowledge of finance and investments. He was convinced that he should be able to learn from him. For a while he went to Switzerland on errands for Jack. Trevor bought gold in the form of sovereigns and Krugerands. He invested money in Swiss banks. It all petered out after a few years and my impression was that he lost rather than made money. There was certainly no jubilation and the whole escapade was quietly dropped.

Trevor's second problem with money was that he yearned for all the luxuries in life. Having no occupation, he spent money out of boredom. He loved small gadgets: cameras and dinky radios. Eventually he would tire of these purchases and give them away to make way for something new. Trevor told me the story of how a London cab driver had thrown a sixpenny tip back at Grandpa who simply picked up his money unabashed. Of course, my grandfather had lived his whole life in the North where expectations were lower than in the city. Nevertheless, there was a lack of appreciation that other people needed an income to live. On his travels, Trevor praised the efficiency of the Swiss trains and the cleanliness of the streets in more affluent societies. On returning home, he criticised everything British. He bemoaned the often-dilapidated state of Heathrow's terminal buildings and the litter in the London streets. I found it difficult to agree with his criticism of British workers and the poor service in Britain given he had worked so little himself.

With inherited capital, the Hares never needed to pay a mortgage. Granny had money of her own from her family, which she kept invested in the stock market. Barbara also had her own money, separate to the housekeeping money that Alastair gave her. So, if Barbara ever wanted something for herself, she did not have to ask her husband for money. Trevor was a frivolous and social being. He had been born with money and privilege. He had little time for either compassion or morality. He enjoyed making fun of others: the Jews, the Blacks and the Americans were all targets. Racism was quite acceptable in the Hare family and I was always shocked by the use of the word nigger. I could not interpret the term as anything other than hugely offensive. When I considered my own sense of self, I did not see that I would feel any different if I had been born in Africa, China or even in different social circumstances in my own country. It seemed to me that where we are born is simply a lottery.

Another favourite topic was 'when I am gone'. This centred around his assurances that he would not have much money to leave us when he died. Proudly, I used to assure him that I would be able to provide for myself and that he did not need to worry about me. It was not at all evident to me that there would be any money left by the time he had spent his way through it. Occasionally it was tempting to contemplate the prospect of an inheritance and even to resent Trevor's ability to throw away everything he had. However, when I looked at my father's life and problems, I wondered whether it was such an advantage to inherit money. I certainly did not believe that children have a right to expect their parents' money.

I grew up feeling that I had control of my own destiny. I appreciated being free of the impediment of wealthy parents wanting to control all my choices. However, it was sometimes difficult not to be frustrated by Trevor's lack of understanding of our situation. He was a tremendous snob. He seemed to think he deserved to be born into a rich family. He thought it equally natural that others live in poverty. I had none of the money he had grown up with. My grandmother had paid for our education but no more than that.

Trevor complained to Jo that his parents used money as a means of control. He had grown up to be dependent on hand-outs but he only got money if he complied with his parents' wishes. The Hares refused to accept the medical school's conclusion that Trevor was not suited to a career in medicine. They insisted he continue his studies. Jo told me her belief that Frank's saying "any fool can be a doctor" undermined his son's confidence and contributed to his sense of failure. Trevor felt that his parents put him down continuously. It was certainly true that he was always convinced that he was a failure. This of course was a self-fulfilling belief since personal confidence is so often vital to success in any enterprise.

Trevor was never stuffy despite being older. As I reached teenage years, he grew a short bristly moustache and had a large potbelly. He had a casual style of dress. He wore blue jeans and sweaters from Marks and Spencer. All this changed when he went up North. Jo described this effect on his personality: *"After he cleaned me up, he went up to see his mother and father to get their blessing. This was the only time that I sensed something wrong. The day he went to Durham to meet his parents Trevor went upstairs to change and came down a different person. It was not only his clothes, which were ones he would not normally be seen dead in. It was his personality that had changed; I did not know him."*

Jo often dwelled on the negatives and perhaps she had good reason to. I never had to live with Trevor. Certainly, his friends saw the best of him. He had a number of lifelong friends, which not many people can say. There were the negatives from his social class. But as a father who I saw a few times a year, I found him very personable. He always seemed pleased to see us even as adults. It was very enjoyable to spend an evening together. We kept in touch by phone, not as a regular duty but when we had something to say or to keep in touch. I wished that I had known him better but there was a generation gap as well as a social gap. Perhaps it was best that I did not know too much about the father I loved from childhood.

# PART VI: OUT IN THE WORLD

## Sixth form college and meeting boys at last

I left QAS in the summer of 1977 when I was sixteen. On the last day of term, Sarah and I took the train to London. Trevor was taking us to Italy with Alan. I thought it was ironic that we were going to Ischia, where my parents spent their honeymoon. I was curious to see it and wondered if Trevor intended the trip to indicate to us that his relationship with Alan was for the longer term. Perhaps he just wanted us all to get to know each other better. The holiday got off to a slow start because unusually we had to wait in the airport for 7 hours before we managed to get staff standby seats. From Rome, we caught a train to Naples and then a boat to Ischia.

We stayed in the port of Forio in a hotel with a pool. Forio is a small, Mediterranean port with picturesque old buildings and small shops selling tourist souvenirs and fresh produce. Sarah complained to me that she did not like Alan. She rarely said a word when we were with them. It was equally evident that Trevor and Alan wanted time alone. Sarah and I spent our days on the beach or by the pool. I was flattered when the Italian boys tried to chat me up on the beach or as we were walking along. They became annoying after a while and I pretended to be German or French as a joke to test their determination and challenge their language skills.

In the evenings, the four of us joined the other tourists and locals promenading up and down the main street lined with cafés and bars. Later we ate at one of the outdoor restaurants. I noticed that Alan tended to drink too fast and that he got drunk easily. One day Trevor asked Alan to take us over to the mainland to visit Pompeii. Another day we went with him to the island of Capri to visit the Blue Grotto. On the way back home, we had one night in Rome. We went to a restaurant for dinner where the service was very slow. Trevor announced that we were going to leave. As we left there was a commotion as the waiters shouted and gesticulated. Trevor liked to insist on his rights. I have also found that embarrassment does not stop me, as an adult, from complaining when I feel cheated.

I was looking forward to living at home with my mother for the first time in my life. However, as the time approached, I became increasingly apprehensive about how the year would turn out. I wondered how we would get on together because we quite frequently disagreed over Simon's behaviour. Jo worked hard as a single parent but inevitably, she was accustomed to running her family alone without needing to justify her actions to anyone. She would take short cuts and go with the flow to make things easier. I thought that Simon was losing out in the sense of personal standards and discipline. I felt that my relationship with Jo was strong enough for us to be able to discuss the matter objectively.

As a child, I had enjoyed listening to Jo's experiences and views on the world. Now I was starting to have opinions of my own. I had hoped for an unbiased soul mate in discussing topics. But increasingly I met with defensiveness. She had made her choices and could neither justify nor change her approach. From her perspective, she felt criticised. Jo explained that during her adolescence she had had a chip on her shoulder. She used to overreact to everything that was said to her. She said that since all teenagers are unreasonable, she would ignore my comments. I was naturally frustrated by this. A few times I was tempted to walk out and slam the door but doing so would only have proved her point.

I had never met Jo's father, my grandfather, and I was curious to meet him. I asked Tommy if he would take Sarah and me over to Yateley see him. Disappointingly my grandfather Ernest said very little to us. Later Tommy explained that his father had assumed we were Tommy's daughters (although Tommy only had one daughter). Probably our upper-class accents didn't help. On the way back, I asked Tommy what I should do about Jo's reluctance to correct Simon's behaviour. Tommy advised me to leave Jo to bring up Simon by herself. His view was that I was the stranger coming to live in their family. I could see that he was right but it hurt me to accept that I was just a visitor even in my mother's home.

I was worried about how I would survive at sixth form college. I desperately wanted to be popular and to be found attractive by the boys. I was not naturally talented at making myself up and I spent a great deal of time worrying about what I looked like. I was depressed because I felt that I was so different to everyone else. I decided that I looked too serious in glasses. I thought that I would be more successful with boys and making friends if I looked more attractive. I persuaded Trevor to buy me some hard contact lenses, which were significantly cheaper than the soft ones. When I first got them, I spent hours crying with frustration in front of the mirror trying to put them in. It felt as if I was putting grit into my eyes.

Sarah and I had been invited to Feri's house in Scotland for a New Year's party. We took the train to London where Trevor told me that he was depressed. The next day Sarah and I flew up to Edinburgh and Feri's father came to pick us up from the airport. It was New Year's Eve and there was a live band with Scottish dancing. We had learned many Scottish dances at The Sneep. The Gay Gordons and Strip the Willow brought back memories of our school days. I enjoyed flirting with the boys our age who were friends of the family. I spent time imagining that they might find me attractive. During this year, I went occasionally to Reading to visit Sarah at QAS. One time I met Alison, who had also left QAS, and we went to the cinema in Reading with Feri, Sarah and Alison's sister Caroline. Sarah always phoned home on a regular basis.

I struggled at college because all three subjects had a significantly different syllabus to the course I had studied in the first year at QAS. In January there were mock exams. I was dismayed by my results, which were 38% for Chemistry, 55% for Maths and 33% for Physics. I knew these grades were low but I was third in the group for Physics. So there seemed to be hope that my marks might improve before the public exams. This was a much less rigorous academic environment compared with QAS and it was difficult to know how to interpret my results. I decided that I could only do my best. I did not see what else I could do. On my seventeenth birthday in March, I applied for my provisional driving license. Driving lessons cost £3.50 a week for an hour. By spending money on nothing else I paid for my own lessons, which I really enjoyed. I was a little nervous at first when I was getting used to the manual gears. But driving felt very natural and gave me a sense of freedom.

In the Easter holidays, Sarah and I planned a cycling trip to Winchester. Jo had no problem with us setting off on our own. As we were now teenagers, our parents rarely tried to stop us doing whatever we wanted. We grew up with the freedom to make our own choices and in that we were more advantaged than many of our peers. The mother of one family I met through school, insisted on accompanying her teenage daughters to the toilet every time when visiting someone else's house. We set off on the first day for the twenty-mile ride to Winchester. We planned to travel for some days. We had rucksacks and some money to stay in youth hostels.

The trip got off to a bad start. We hadn't checked the weather forecast and on the first day, it poured with rain. We had no waterproof clothing so we both got soaked through. Sarah wanted to turn back but I was determined to carry on. After hours of cycling in the rain, we arrived in Winchester and stayed overnight in the youth hostel. Everything we were wearing was soaked through. We had no change of clothing so we spent the evening steaming in front of a gas fire. The next morning, we were woken very early by a loud wake-up bell. Together with the other residents we had to contribute to the chores of running the hostel as part-payment for our stay. We had both had enough and decided to return home.

I went for an interview at college about going to university. I was still set on medicine because nothing had happened to change my mind. Neither Jo nor Trevor had expressed any interest in the decision so I completed my university entry forms myself. I received a provisional offer from Southampton and visited the medical school. By now I was used to making my own decisions. Later in the year, Jo came to one of my college parent's evenings. I was annoyed because she had no knowledge of the academic process and she had never taken any interest in my progress before. There did not seem much point in her becoming involved at this late stage in my school life. I thought that it would have been more appropriate for the teachers to give me the feedback directly.

St Mary's College was in Basingstoke, about ten miles from Kingsclere. There was a short walk down the hill to the bus stop and then a thirty-minute bus ride to Basingstoke. The college was a further twenty-minute walk through the town. One of the first adjustments I had to make was to get out of the habit of standing up every time a teacher walked into the classroom. It also came as quite a shock at 16 to be suddenly mixed in with boys. I was self-conscious of my public-school accent and single sex education. I was also aware that in arriving halfway through the sixth form, the others had already formed their social groups. The vast majority of them had come from the same state school the year before.

There were only two other girls in my physics group so I was naturally included on a table with Caroline and Sian. I was relieved that both girls were friendly despite my shyness. Caroline was interesting to talk to but she was not popular with the rest of the year. I was much more pleased when Sian walked out of college with me because she was part of the group who had all gone to the local state school together. They represented the popular crowd and I aspired to be as socially confident and 'normal' as they were.

## Concerns about being accepted and an infatuation

During a physics lesson, a boy called Tim introduced himself to our table of three girls. At lunchtime we all went down to the pub together for half a pint of larger. I felt self-conscious of how young and immature I must appear to the others who were all a year older than I was. Over the next few days, I became aware that Tim was making special effort towards me. He started talking to me in lessons and he walked down to the bus station with me. I realised that I was getting onto dangerous ground. Tim was good-looking and pleasant enough but I felt no particular attraction towards him.

I was not sure how I was supposed to feel about a boyfriend but I did not enjoy talking to Tim any more than to anyone else. I was also getting attention from some of the other boys so I wanted to keep my options open. On Tim's birthday, it was agreed that Caroline, Sian and I would go with him to the pub. But the other two girls dropped out and feeling totally betrayed by my friends, I was left in the awkward situation of going to the pub with Tim on my own. Over lunch, he asked me to go out with him on a date to the cinema. I didn't know how I could say "no" politely so I accepted his invitation. I was taking the easy route (at least to begin with) but I also wondered, partly to justify my deceit, whether I should give Tim a chance by trying to get to know him better.

Later I concluded that attraction is usually immediate, if at all. Each step in a courtship, where one person proposes and the other accepts, is part of a journey towards a relationship. Each step a person makes towards that end goal is taken as confirmation by the other person that their feelings are reciprocated. I concluded that if a woman is not attracted to a man, then continuing to accept invitations is misleading. Tim and I went first to see a movie and then to the pub. Tim was pleasant but I didn't feel at ease talking to him. I was conscious of the struggle to make conversation.

Tim was quite serious. He did not lark around like some of the others. He didn't make me feel admired. I did not think of him romantically. I was careful to avoid any hint of physical proximity during our date that might be misinterpreted as a willingness to kiss. Now that we had been on a date together, everyone at college was openly referring to us as a couple. Tim continued to come and talk to me in breaks. It must be very difficult for men to differentiate between natural female timidity and a total lack of interest. Women are rarely willing to reject a man and expose themselves to conflict.

Some of the other boys who paid me attention were not as sensible as Tim was. They joked and play-acted in a flirtatious way, which was amusing and flattering. Richard was one of these. He was tall, dark haired and had an adolescent's bad complexion. He was popular with the rest of the year-group. Richard and I sat at the same table in Chemistry lessons. From early on he acted the gallant flatterer by saying that I was marvellous. This flattery and the attention he gave me, contributed to the attraction. I certainly felt no erotic interest in his body or any carnal desire as I assume boys do. I rarely thought of intercourse at all. It was more of an emotional desire to feel loved and admired. For a while, he accompanied me back from Maths lessons. He was obviously trying to impress and I found myself falling for his charm. Once Richard walked out of college with me and asked me to come to a party. I agreed to go but I was depressed that he thought I was still with Tim. I resolved to tell Tim that I did not want to go out with him.

I did not know what I could do to indicate that I was not attracted to Tim romantically without hurting his feelings. To back off from the perception of a developing relationship I decided that the only thing to do was to avoid meeting him. But everyone kept leaving us together. One day I had to walk down into town with Tim but I avoided showing any friendliness. On another day, I could not get out of going into town at lunchtime with him but I turned down his invitation to go to the pub. I didn't have the maturity or the emotional detachment to explain how I felt. I lacked the courage and the experience to know what to say and how to say it. I concluded the whole business was a mess. I felt deceitful but I decided that I just had to leave Tim to figure it out. Eventually, I noticed that he had finally taken the hint. Of course, I should have been more open with him. But I didn't want to hurt his feelings.

One weekend Richard called me and invited me to his house. His mother had to come and fetch me because they lived miles away. His parents went out in the afternoon so we had the house to ourselves. We sat in his bedroom and listened to his records. I was intimidated by his familiarity with contemporary music and politics through the lyrics of these songs. The problem was that Richard was always witty and humorous. This made me feel self-conscious because I could never think of anything to say to him. But despite being alone, Richard's manner never changed. He never attempted to talk seriously and I was too timid to initiate any conversation. Our interaction involved uncomfortably fooling around together.

Richard must have been in a similar situation. He didn't have the experience to know how to break down the initial reserve that exists between two people. This is made worse when each person is anxious. As we gain experience, we feel more at ease just being ourselves. At the time I was overwhelmed by my sense of inadequacy and felt utterly helpless to respond to him. Afterwards I was depressed because I had been quiet with his family. Richard's mother was the headmistress of Simon's primary school in Kingsclere. Jo used to help at the school. I was self-conscious that his mother must have known that Jo was poor and uneducated. My public-school education seemed irrelevant to me now that I lived with Jo. But Richard may have been intimidated by my accent and my serious disposition. Men gain more confidence to persevere once they have more experience of women. Naturally, some men are much more confident about approaching women than others.

I looked forward to seeing Richard at college. I hoped that we might be more relaxed with each other given he had invited me to his house. But the awkwardness continued. Presumably, Richard lacked confidence as I did and the fooling around continued. I started to feel that more people knew about us. I hoped that he would not go off me. The next weekend, I was praying that Richard would call all weekend. I instinctively expected him to make all the effort. I was too proud to talk about my feelings with the other girls, who might have helped communicate with Richard. Over the half-term break I felt depressed as I realised, I did not have any friends to go around with. I also wondered whether I should have some hobbies so that I would be more interesting and have something to talk about. I was self-conscious about how quiet and uninteresting I must appear. I never knew what to say to all of Richard's friends.

After half term, I did not get on with Richard too well. Sometimes I even thought he was rude and I vowed that I would never speak to him again. Other times he would ignore me. Then suddenly he would talk to me as a normal person or even fool around as if he still liked me. I could not find a way of interacting with him that felt natural. Our interaction was always dependent on him making the first move, which he did ostentatiously and in public. If he had interacted in a more relaxed manner, told me about himself and asked questions of me, perhaps we could have got to know each other. Feeling that I had to respond in a flamboyant or amusing way just left me tongue-tied. I, of course, did absolutely nothing to help.

Richard was part of the popular group who all knew each other from the local state school. They sat around in breaks together, chatting or playing cards. They also played Postman's Knock. I understood that the game involved flirting or kissing, so I kept well clear. I was constantly depressed about being a social failure and dreaded going into college. I tried to be friendly with Richard but decided that he was no longer keen on me. I could not blame him. I noted that he was not always rude but I was giving up hope. One time, Richard put his arm around me and strangled me. Another time, he caught up with me and walked down into Basingstoke with me. I was wishing that we would either get somewhere in our relationship or not, either way. Richard talked about liking another girl and I accepted that I had done nothing to encourage him. I was giving up hope for Richard ever wanting to ask me out again.

During one party I went to, I noted that Richard was very quiet. I wanted to make some effort. I tried to catch his eye but failed. I gave Richard a Christmas card but felt humiliated when he ignored me. Richard did not invite me to his birthday party in December. There was so much uncertainty in our interaction that there was more pain than pleasure. Whenever something nice happened, I was euphoric and the world seemed so bright. When things went wrong, I felt as if the world was coming to an end. I was invited to one girl's party and her brother flirted with me. He asked why I was always so quiet, which sent me into the depths of depression again.

Jo was no help. She was struggling with her own dating difficulties. I went with her to one of her divorcee social evenings and she just stood on the side by herself. I decided that she was more of a wallflower than I was. After a parents' evening, Jo told me that the Chemistry teacher described me as 'shy and retiring', which depressed me even more. By April Richard was still making effort towards me. He was always mucking about and was never serious. He asked whether he could dance with me in Chemistry but I refused. I was unsure whether he was flattering me or making fun of me. Despite the strength of my emotions, I decided that my feelings for Richard must be an infatuation. I never really knew him so it could not count as love. In May, I continued to be besotted with Richard but heard that he was going out with Sue. In June, I noted that Richard came and talked to me once in Basingstoke.

I think the problem was that I didn't know if he was sincere. I didn't know whether to take him seriously. He never opened up and said what he was interested in or what he wanted in life. Neither did he show any interest in me as a person. So we never got to know each other. Some people are political and their priority is maintaining a public profile that impresses others. For me it has always been important to talk with someone about important issues so that I can understand what kind of person they are. This is how I come to trust them. There was no doubt that he was attracted to me but if he wasn't prepared to be honest then I couldn't trust him. Women often talk about trust and men find this difficult to understand.

# Au-pairing in a chateau and vineyard in France

By the middle of June, I had finished my exams. I decided to go to France for the summer to learn French. Trevor had always admired anyone who could speak languages. I hadn't studied French since I started my A level courses two years previously but I was curious to see if I could use the language I had learned at school. I did not have any contacts in France or anyone who could give me advice on what to do. Jo suggested looking in The Lady magazine so I bought a copy. I found that there were not many opportunities for someone as young as seventeen. Most of the advertisements wanted girls who were at least eighteen and many jobs asked for a driving license. I applied to some agencies advertised in the back pages.

A few weeks later, I received a letter from a French woman with an aristocratic sounding name. Madame told me that she had seven children but six of these were already grown up and married. She was looking for an au pair to help her in the house. This was the only lead I had, so I wrote back and accepted. I asked Trevor to get me one of his £10 staff return tickets to Bordeaux. I left for France immediately after the exams ended at the end of June in 1978. I arrived in Bordeaux and took the train to Bergerac as I had been instructed. The husband, a kindly man in his sixties, came to meet me at the station. After practising on the train journey, I managed to say "Je m'appele Jane" as Monsieur came towards me. Monsieur made a few attempts at conversation during the half hour drive south to Castillonnes but my ability to respond was limited.

They lived in a large chateau, which was a few kilometres from Castillonnes, a small village in the Dordogne. The house had spacious rooms, high ceilings and impressive decor. The main rooms had tapestries hanging on the walls and antique furniture. My room was up in what felt like the servants' quarters because the rooms were small. I had a handover from a French girl who had been working for the family for a few months but was now leaving. She had been in a juvenile care institution before getting the job. I surmised that Madame employed the cheapest labour she could find. This girl had worked in the fields and we picked courgettes. Madame wanted me to do housework and other jobs in the house.

I started work at eight in the morning and was on duty all day until dinner was cleared at 9 o'clock at night. The good news was that lunch and dinner were essentially free time when I sat and listened to the French spoken at the table. I helped serve at mealtimes. I also cleared plates and helped with the washing up. There was a dishwasher and two large sinks. This was the first time I came across the concept of rinsing plates. In Jo's sink, we just piled all the dirty plates in together and washed the whole meal's worth of crockery in the same water. Madame removed all the food first and then had a sink of clean water to rinse the plates in before drying. In a house with many guests, there was always hours of ironing to be done.

The chateau seemed to be self-sufficient in much of the food that was served at the dining table. I was sometimes asked to help in the fields by harvesting vegetables. I also helped the old peasant woman who lived on the grounds of the chateau. She was difficult to understand at first because she spoke a local dialect but she had a good sense of humour. There were rabbits in cages as well as ducks and chickens roaming about the farm buildings. I helped with the slaughter of a duck once. This experience convinced me later to be vegetarian, not because I was horrified by killing but, simply because I could not justify killing such magnificent animals when it was possible to be vegetarian. The chateau had its own vineyards and so we drank red wine at every meal. But meals lasted such a long time that we didn't get drunk. Madame also made her own grenadine fruit syrup that we made up into a delicious cordial drink.

I worked all day on instructions from Madame. She made little conversation. Her sole focus appeared to be ensuring that I was fully employed. I came to accept that if I finished a job early, she just invented something new. When she ran out of jobs for me, she asked me to start cleaning the windows of the chateau. I made a conscious decision to take my time. One of Sarah's school friends, Nicky lived nearby. One day she came with her mother and Alice (who had been cracked on me). I was in the front hallway with my mop and bucket when they arrived. I was conscious of looking like a servant. I decided that the experience was good for my humility.

Madame also took in paying guests. These were children sent by their parents to learn French. Alexander was thirteen. Madame left his entertainment mainly up to me so I am not sure that his French improved much. A German girl, Kirsten, arrived and another English boy, Robert, who was also thirteen. The two English boys were hard work as they were often fighting about something. My own French was fluent by the time I left. I hadn't enjoyed learning French at school but I seemed to have an ear for the language when in the country. I bought some detective novels as light reading, which improved my grammar. I learned the use of the subjunctive and also some French slang that their daughter often used. My reading reinforced the language that I was learning during the day.

After a couple of weeks, two English lads arrived to work with me at the chateau. Paul was 21 and had just finished his degree at Sheffield University. Paul had a moustache and a northern (England) accent. He found the adjustment to life on the chateau difficult at first. It was a culture shock and he had very little ability to communicate. His knowledge of French was very basic and he did not pick up the language easily. He was impressed with my French that I had acquired from my two-week head start. Madame just gave out orders and did not take into account that young people miss their friends and freedom. There was no social life at the chateau. I did my best to reassure Paul that the place was not as bad as it might seem at first and we spent most of our free time together.

Paul and I used to sit together outside in the evenings after dinner and drink the chateau wine. James arrived a week later. He was 19 and studying for his A levels in languages at boarding school. James sometimes joined in with our evening socialising but he was not talkative and seemed happier keeping to himself. I was pleased that I got on with everyone, both French and English. On Sundays we went into the nearest village, Castillonnes. There were no buses so we had to walk or hitchhike a few kilometres, which could be an adventure. Everything was shut apart from the church and the cafes.

One of the real benefits of the job was that we all ate together in the large dining hall. Lunch lasted for at least two hours and dinner for at least three. There was always salad and fresh baguette. Madame was an excellent cook and did all the cooking herself. The food was superb and served in several courses. There was always dessert, a pudding with a selection of cheeses afterwards. I had Petit-Suisse for the first time. These were small portions of fromage frais, rather like a very thick yogurt. A favourite dish of mine was courgettes farcies. The courgettes were stuffed with mincemeat, breadcrumbs, onions and herbs and baked in the oven. Sadly I never had the opportunity to learn from Madame. My job was making the salad dressing with Dijon mustard, wine vinegar and olive oil. Over the summer, there were few days without guests. Different members of the family came over the summer with their children. Their eldest son lived in Belgium and visited with his wife and young children.

At table, conversation was always in French and we took part where we could. At first, I didn't understand a word but after a month, I was starting to understand a little of what was said. Monsieur was a charming man and once my French improved, he would occasionally engage in some jovial commentary that I never quite understood. When in a light-hearted mood, he liked to sing the phrase "cettes jeunes filles Anglaises" from a traditional French song that included much inuendo towards me. He was a charming flirt but he never made me feel uncomfortable. He complained to his wife that she worked me "comme un neigre!" but he never interfered. Their youngest daughter was fourteen. She was pretty, with long blond hair. I took exception to her precociousness early on and tried to ignore her because of her condescending attitude.

My first payday was 31st July when I finally received FF250 (around $40 for a month's work), which was not very much even then. There was very little free time but equally nowhere to go when I was off duty. Madame was also in her sixties. I don't remember her having a personality. I don't think she had a sense of humour. She was simply my employer. She appeared to see me simply as someone she was paying to do work for her. Madame told me that even on Sundays I had to go down to the kitchen to start work as usual at 8 o'clock. On the first Sunday, I deliberately ignored this instruction because it seemed ridiculous not to have one morning off. She never said anything and I continued to lie in on Sundays.

Paul's job was to look after the horses the family kept. I do not remember anyone riding them but I was not interested in horses. I would sometimes go out to the stable to help Paul or to chat to him while he worked. Like me, he had no experience of horses but he learned how to feed them and muck out the stables. James's job was feeding the snails. They were fed on dried macaroni and it was James's job to clean out their cages. Otherwise, the boys were asked to help with various practical projects. There were several cottages on the estate, which the parents had donated to their children. The boys helped with the building and renovation work on the cottages.

Paul was easy to talk to but I was not attracted to him. I was relieved that he never made a pass at me. Sometimes I wondered because we spent so much time together talking. Whatever Paul's feelings were, he never gave any indication of them while we spent long hours together. While I was in France, I learned how to masturbate. I didn't set out to discover orgasm. It just happened. I could have discovered masturbation the year before. But I didn't. I concluded that I had matured sexually to the point where my responsiveness surfaced. I also had the experience later in life that the emotional sensations of being in love drown out any ability to respond to eroticism. I had no source of erotic literature while I was in France. But I had scenarios that I could draw on from my past reading.

I had always had a natural comfort position of rocking my hips from side to side while thinking about sleep. My first attempts at masturbation were a variation on the same activity but included a conscious decision to combine thinking about a sexual scenario and pushing my fingers over my clit and into the tissue either side of my labia. The resulting sexual release was delightful, a true pleasure but not so overwhelming that I felt that the experience defined the whole meaning to life. I could happily wait for the next morning (if time) or evening to continue exploring my new private discovery.

I only knew that it was masturbation because I had read about the possibility. In my own mind, I thought of the activity as 'touching myself'. This best described what felt like just rubbing rhythmically over my vulva. The term masturbation (certainly in the context of male masturbation) sounded much more sexually explicit than what I did. I never felt an urgent need to masturbate and usually did so when going to sleep. My fantasies were based on books I had read. Otherwise I imagined being in an institution where men were free to do various exploratory sensual and sexual things to my body. Over time I invested in finding new scenarios for masturbation.

# Taking time out to learn about working life

In August Trevor rang to tell me my exam results. I had achieved only two C grades and a D in physics. I needed a minimum of three B grades for medicine. The option to retake was not a realistic one. My A level years had been emotionally painful. I could not face going back to the sixth form again even though I was young enough to spend the time. Most medical schools did not accept retakes anyway. I decided to take my results as an act of fate and concluded that I was not destined to become a doctor. I asked Trevor to put my application through the clearing process for biochemistry, which I had found interesting at college. Trevor wrote by return:

*The results may not be what you hoped for but they are good nevertheless. However, I found out that the biochemistry course at Southampton is now fully booked and I would not know where to start from there. It would seem that there is no hurry to leave France now. Also, that you seem to have a year to consider your position and to view your choices. You could take your chance to better your French, then you could find some way to do a cookery course or a secretarial course.... If you are set on biochemistry and I don't even know what that is, then you could try for a lab job in that line. There is nursing, medical secretary..."*

I thought it was typical that at the first sign of failure he should imply that I should settle for a non-graduate career. Over the coming weeks, I decided that I would take a year off and I considered what I might do with the year. Fashionable pursuits were grape picking or working as a chalet girl in the Alps. Trevor wrote with his advice:

*"I don't think I can give you much advice. Just do what you want. It may be a great experience to go grape picking and to have a young man to guard you so long as he does that. Don't drink too much and stay always in control of situations. Remember if it comes to the crunch you can always make young men very happy very easily if they get randy but always keep your legs crossed!! You will think me very rude but save it for the right one!! ... I don't think I mind what you do so long as you take care of yourself. You are both extremely beautiful girls and I hope with your education you will do well for yourselves. During this year, you will have*

*time to do and see lots of things to help you decide future plans. No need to aim too high academically, medicine would be fine but it is a long haul 5-6 years. It may be better to pick an easier way to make a living and in the long run find a man with the right position to keep you in the style to which you would wish to be!!!"*

I appreciated his humour but also thought it was typical that he should revert to stereotypes. He had appeared to be keen to suggest that I could become a sexual woman and enjoy sex for itself. But in the end, he appeared to accept that women are fundamentally not sexually driven. His two closest relatives, his mother and sister, were the least overtly sexual women you could imagine. But despite all his travels and the diversity of social and sexual situations he must have witnessed, he had concluded that women use men for sex. My own conclusions were essentially the same even as a virgin at the age of 17. I did not see women of any background or age demonstrating the same interest in eroticism that many men did.

I left France in September 1978 after a stay of three months. I concluded that the experience would not be one that I would have volunteered for if I knew what it would involve. But having survived it, I had learned a great deal. I was very pleased that I had managed to learn to speak basic French fairly fluently. Paul and I kept in touch as friends. At the end of my gap year, I met my first boyfriend David in the South of France. I did not know how to write to Paul explaining that I now had a boyfriend. Although we had only been friends, I felt awkward telling him I had a boyfriend in a letter.

Paul came to visit me in my first term at Southampton University. David and I were in my room when Paul arrived unexpectedly. I introduced them but David's attitude was off hand. He was ill-humoured in a territorial kind of way and carried on reading his newspaper. Paul was equally ill-at-ease. It was very awkward. Through lack of experience, I didn't think to offer to go somewhere with Paul to talk privately. I wanted to explain the situation honestly but I felt I couldn't with both of them there. It was a shame but in the end the result was probably the same. Paul never wrote again after that. I can only assume that he wanted a more serious relationship all the time but had never had the courage to say so.

On my return from France, I went to a careers advisory service. After taking some tests I was told that I would be well suited to a career as a pharmacist or as an optician. My instincts told me that I wanted a more ambitious career. I had failed to qualify for a medical degree but with A levels in Maths, Physics and Chemistry, I was sure that if I had been male, I would have been directed towards more highly paid jobs such as engineering or computing. I wanted to be able to support myself and I was not prepared to accept a lower income just because I was female. I concluded that the safest route was to study a subject at university that I enjoyed. Maths was the obvious choice. A Maths degree didn't have the same prestige as medicine but it might open up other graduate careers later on when I had a clearer idea of what I wanted to do.

I decided to look for temporary work in the UK. I was still yearning for a normal home life after years away at boarding school. I thought that I would travel again later in the year. I hoped that getting a job in the UK and a few months at home might be a good experience. I signed on with various employment agencies and was dismayed to find that my A levels were of little value to me. All that anyone wanted to know was whether I could type. Academic qualifications evidently did not substitute for work experience. I got a job as an accounts clerk at Klix, a division of Mars, in Basingstoke.

I was going to catch the bus to work but Maureen's boyfriend, Jeff, volunteered to drive me on his way to work. Jeff was pleasant enough but I always found conversation difficult. I had offered to contribute towards the cost of petrol at the start of the arrangement but Jeff refused to accept any money. Later, I stupidly asked again if I could do something for him to repay him for my share of the petrol cost. Jeff suggested that I could come to his house and do some housework. Lesson number one: if a man will not accept a fair money contribution towards costs then accept his generosity. Lesson number two: never agree to go to a single man's house by yourself (particularly in the evening) without expecting trouble.

I was very aware of the likely direction of the evening when I arrived at his house and started on his housework. After an hour or so, Jeff got out the whisky bottle and invited me to join him. His comments were becoming more suggestive but I was confident of my ability to drink whisky without becoming incapable. After a fair amount of whisky had been consumed, the doorbell rang. It was Jo at the door asking for me. I was acutely embarrassed partly because of her appearance as a chaperone but also because she was drunk. Within a few minutes, Jeff had his arms around her and they were kissing.

I knew that he was just taunting me with my unwillingness to oblige him. I decided to leave them to it and went home. Minutes later the doorbell rang. I was reluctant to answer because I did not want to let this man into the house. I couldn't see another option so I opened the door and helped Jeff lift Jo upstairs and into bed. This left me with a spare man in the living room to deal with. Jeff now embarked on persuading me to have sex with him. When I turned him down, he jibed me with being sexless and a coward. However, there was no way I was going to have sex with just any man. Luckily, he eventually tired of trying and left without an unpleasant scene.

From the daily bus rides to college, I knew a girl called Sue who was studying for secretarial exams. She was shy and under-confident perhaps because of her large build. She persuaded me to accompany her to weekly bell-ringing classes at the village church. One evening some bell-ringers from another church came to visit and we all went to the pub afterwards for a drink. Sue was flattered when one of the men took an interest in her. She and I had a couple of drinks with this man and his friend in the bar. It was evident that Sue was intent on getting into a sexual situation. She asked me to go along with them in the car as a safety measure. After a couple of miles and in the middle of nowhere, Sue and her companion asked me and the other guy if we would leave them alone in the car.

Sue reassured me that she was happy to be left alone to have sex with this stranger. I was not pleased to be stranded with a man I had only just met in a country lane with no streetlighting. I knew that the man was a policeman and engaged to be married. I hoped that his profession meant that he was honourable and that his engagement would hold him back from any sexual advances. My mother had not given me much advice about men but she had recommended that if in doubt I should hold hands with a man on a date. So, I held hands with this man and felt ridiculous. But who knows perhaps it worked. It may have communicated naivety and immaturity, which might deter some men. We walked slowly back to the village, making polite conversation, and we parted amicably.

I had kept in touch with Alison after we left Queen Anne's. She went to a private day school near her parent's home. I stayed overnight with Alison and felt sorry for her because her parents treated her like a child. She was not even allowed to travel by train on her own. Alison talked about Philippe her Spanish boyfriend and I told her about Richard. Alison and I applied for jobs in the Harrods sale. We went for an interview in London and both got jobs. Alison sold bags and gloves from behind a counter. My job was assisting in the Evening and After Six department, which sold women's evening wear. I had little interest in clothes and certainly no knowledge to help a prospective buyer. We had to stand around all day trying to look helpful and I vowed never again to work on a shop floor. To begin with, I stayed at Alison's house in Bracknell and we travelled up to London each day by train with her father.

For the last week, I stayed with a friend of Alan's. I had met Jenny in Zeals. She left a copy of the erotic novel The Story of O lying around and I asked if I could read it. It provided a number of passages that I was able to use for orgasm. She was the only woman I have met who was relaxed about admitting to reading erotica. She had a high-earning job as a buyer of children's clothes for a well-known national store. During my stay we never talked about anything intimate. In fact I have never met a woman who was willing to be explicit or open about her sexual experiences. The few women who do comment, do so by using bravado or making a joke. Perhaps my serious nature doesn't encourage confidences. Yet men are never criticised for being too serious. It seems as if everyone expects women to be always smiling and amenable.

Towards the end of my gap year, I worked as an au pair in the South of France. While I was there, Alison called to ask if I would help her get an au pair job. I met her at the airport and took her to the agency in Nice that I had used. They found her a job and I did not hear from her for two or three weeks. Then I got a call. She had left her job and set off on her own hitchhiking. She had gone to stay with the man who gave her a lift. She told me that they were going to get married. I could not believe what she was telling me after just a couple of weeks in France. At school, she had been passionate about her crush on Donny Osmond. Then she had spent a whole year talking incessantly about a Spanish boy she met on holiday. Just as some men obsess about body parts, some women's belief in true love stops them choosing a sensible partner.

I heard nothing more from Alison until my return to England when I received a formal invitation from her parents to a wedding reception at their house. I was embarrassed because I felt responsible for my involvement in getting her the job in France. Years later, I had a phone call from Alison. She told me that after marrying, she had two children but her husband was promiscuous from the beginning. Finally, she left him because she realised that he was the kind of man who would always be having affairs with other women. She brought her children to live with her parents in England. Alison's parents paid school fees for the children. After a few years, Alison remarried and had a second family in her thirties.

One day while I was exploring my father's bookshelves, I noticed some paperbacks on the top shelf that were turned so their spines faced the wall. They were male homosexual erotic novels. I browsed through a couple and found them easy reading. They were an interesting contrast to the heterosexual erotica that I was used to. Without women, there weren't the references to female anatomy and feminine moral concerns (about being a slut, for example). It was noticeable that men obtained erotic pleasure from a partner's body. Male homosexual erotica gets to the action quickly, saving much pointless reading. It focuses on male anatomy and a man's enjoyment of his responsiveness. It involves more physical fun and less relationship interaction. I found it refreshing.

The stories were highly effective at arousing me and I used some of them for masturbation throughout the rest of my life. One of them I used regularly for more than 40 years. It referred to women's dislike of the physical and from my own experience, I could relate to this observation. This was contrasted with men's delight in having sexual fun. When I had my own bedroom at Trevor's house, I would take one of these books upstairs, lie on the bed and masturbate in the middle of the day just for fun. As long as I had an effective source of eroticism to use for mental arousal, orgasm was fairly easily and quickly achieved. Looking back, I can't remember the frequency but it may have been daily and possibly more often than that. I mentioned this find to Sarah but I must have been overheard because soon afterwards the books were removed. Trevor and I never referred to the incident, which was a shame. Later I wished that I had asked him for any books he didn't want.

Now that I had discovered masturbation, I naturally made the most of my opportunities to enjoy orgasm. For the most part, I only masturbated when I was in bed. Either in the early morning or before going to sleep. It seemed natural to keep my discovery to myself. It was very personal and no one in my life had ever talked about such personal experiences. When I had asked Sarah about her various love affairs, she had bluntly refused to discuss them. If I was at Kingsclere and Sarah was sleeping on the top bunk, I had to be discrete. The challenge was to masturbate without drawing attention to myself. I found the hip movement caused the bed to sway and I had to supress the sound of my laboured breathing.

## Au-pairing in Germany and rethinking religion

Trevor was finding that London was becoming too expensive. Also, his relationship with Alan was turning out to be one of the most stable he had ever had. Trevor decided to move out to the country to a small village called Zeals in Dorset where he bought a long, thatched cottage just off the main road. The plan was to run a bed and breakfast business. Trevor acted as host and Alan did the cooking, washing and cleaning. Visitors often assumed that they were father and son because of the age difference. Trevor was soon complaining about relatives who expected to stay without paying and I wondered how soon it would be before he charged us. I got on well with Alan during my late teens. He was easy to talk to and we enjoyed philosophising about life. Trevor bought an old mini clubman and Alan volunteered to take me out driving. Alan had passed his driving test at eighteen but he had never had the confidence to drive. Alan was frequently unnerved by my risk-taking but I was pleased later when he started driving himself.

After attending an interview, I had been accepted for a place at Southampton University to study a combined honours course in

Mathematics. Having secured my place for September, I decided to make the most of Trevor's cheap air tickets and go to Germany. Before I left, I applied for various hotel jobs including the Holiday Inn in Frankfurt without any luck. Jo and Sarah told me I should go even though I did not have a job. So, with much apprehension I set off with my return ticket and fifty pounds in my pocket. From the airport, I headed into Frankfurt and found the youth hostel, which was in Sachsenhausen, one of the main nightlife areas. The hostel was open to anyone under the age of 35 and some guests were evidently permanent residents. My money was not going to last very long but at least I had a room for the first couple of nights.

While booking my dormitory bed, I met a friendly American in his thirties called Paul. He invited me to the Irish pub in Sachsenhausen where he was performing as a clown. Being wary of men's motives by now, I decided that his offer was a little too risky for my first night in Frankfurt. I went up to the dormitory room, unpacked and considered reading or going straight to bed. But it felt very boring. It was Saturday night and I was excited by the idea of having the freedom to explore a foreign city. I decided to venture out and at least look in on some nightlife. I found the Irish pub and looking through the window, could see Paul's clown act. I was aware of being only seventeen and I was unwilling to get involved with unknown men in a strange city. I decided not to go into the pub in case I could not disengage myself from the clown. I returned to the hostel, pleased that I had seen some nightlife but returned safely.

The next day I met Paul again and he offered to take me wherever I wanted to go. Over time, I found that he was very difficult to get rid of. He kept following me around and I had the impression that he was lonely. I decided to keep my distance but remain friendly. I like my own company. It leaves gives me the flexibility to do the things that interest me and the opportunity to meet new people. One day when I was passing through Hauptwache underground station, I saw Paul doing his act in the subway shopping mall. It gave me a thrill to think that I knew this man who was doing something so unusual. He had spent his life travelling alone. Once he told me that he knew the Beatles as well as other famous people. I never saw him with friends despite all his boasts of famous connections. Overall, he seemed harmless enough and never made a pass at me.

I went to the Employment Office to try to find hotel work or similar. I soon ran into bureaucratic difficulties because to qualify for work I needed to get a work permit for which I needed a registered address. The youth hostel was not a suitable address and there was no obvious solution. At this point Paul, still pestering daily to accompany me everywhere, offered to take me to the American Club on the Forces Base. There was a chance he could get me a job in the Rotunda Snack Bar there. There were many American army buildings in central Frankfurt at the time. I saw American soldiers everywhere, especially when travelling on the subway trains. Paul escorted me to meet Sergeant Ray who offered me a job as a canteen cleaner once he could get me a work permit.

While I was waiting in the administration office, I got talking to Suzy, who worked there. When Suzy heard that I was living in the youth hostel she invited me to stay with her. I was running out of money, so I was relieved to get an offer of free accommodation. Suzy lived near the base with her husband Chuck, who was a Christian missionary, and seemed to be a safe option. After only three nights at the youth hostel, I moved out with my few belongings and went to live with my new American family. I was out most of the day and reluctant to rely on their hospitality. I had stopped eating because my money was so limited. One morning when I got up, I suddenly went blind for a few seconds, which was quite scary.

I enjoyed working in the canteen. The work was easy. I only had to clear and wipe tables. I was as shy as ever but the other workers were friendly. It was not a glamorous job but at least I could now eat. Suzie knew I wanted to find a German family to stay with, so they talked to German couple they knew who had a one-year-old daughter, Laura. I went to meet Anita and Eberhardt in their three-storey town house in one of Frankfurt's finest residential streets. They were both teachers and spoke excellent English. They were very friendly and educated. As an English teacher on maternity leave, Anita was keen to practise her English. They also wanted someone to baby-sit occasionally during the day and in the evening.

So only a week after arriving in Frankfurt I went to live with Anita and Eberhardt. I was pleased to have found such a nice family who were interesting and who lived in such a lovely home. Most of the time Anita was at home and I helped her in the kitchen peeling or chopping vegetables. For part of the day, Anita sometimes left me on my own with Laura or asked me to take her out in the pushchair. As a couple, they took their parenting role very seriously. This was the first time that I could see the attraction in having a family and trying to raise children as lovingly as they did. A Turkish woman came once a week to clean but Anita asked me to do the ironing.

Anita and Eberhardt were unfailingly generous. I enjoyed the excellent food. Anita used to get up early to cook brioche rolls for breakfast. We ate boiled eggs for breakfast, with fresh bread and home-made jam. Anita was a good cook and she put a lot of thought and effort into preparing healthy meals. Apfelwein (cider) is a Frankfurt speciality that we had on the table each meal with local apple juice and mineral water. We also had German white wine with the evening meal. At weekends Anita served 'Kaffee und Kuchen' often with visitors invited. She made a large fruit tart made with cooked quetchen (plums) or a strawberry flan. When Anita went grocery shopping, there was no apparent budget. My only experience of grocery shopping had been with Jo and she always had to count every penny to know that she could pay. For me at the time, the idea of eating strawberries in such quantities was a luxury.

## The kindness of strangers and thoughts on morality

Anita had studied English Literature at University and she had a house full of books, both German and English. Anita thought every educated person should have read the classics. I had plenty of free time, so I started reading English literature to improve on my education. Anita had just finished work the year before, so she too was enjoying the novelty of having free time to enjoy life. We talked easily together about various topics in the kitchen or in between studying and reading. Anita was interested in women's rights and was the first person to make me aware of the feminist movement.

During the time that I was staying with them, one of Anita and Eberhardt's main interests was their house. I had never appreciated how much thought and effort someone could put into house decoration and furnishings. The living room had wooden floors with rugs and the kitchen was fitted out with modern units. The house had two further floors. I had a bedroom on the top floor, which was their spare room. I was self-conscious of staying in such a model house. I was accustomed to people with money but this was the first time I knew people who had such a conscious sense of style. Anita was attractive and everything she wore was tasteful and expensive. I was surprised to find that, despite their affluence, they considered me privileged simply because of my private education.

During my stay with Anita and Eberhardt, I felt very much in limbo. Up until this point, my life had been preordained for me by adults and split between home and school. I was gradually coming to appreciate just how much I enjoyed studying new topics. I wanted to carry on with my education to degree level. I thought the jobs, I was currently qualified for, would not stretch me intellectually as much as I felt capable of. In the meantime, having so much time to myself provided a unique opportunity to mull over my ideas and conclusions. Life was stretching out before me as a void to be filled somehow. I had time to consider what I wanted to do with my life.

One of the subjects I thought about was religion. I used to pray every night and I read a daily passage from the Bible. Towards the end of my stay, Anita and Eberhardt went away on holiday. I had to stay with Eberhardt's parents in a town about an hour's drive from Frankfurt. They lived in a large town house with a family-run newsagent's shop on the ground floor. While I was staying there, we went to church on Sundays. As I surveyed the congregation participating in this Sunday ritual, I wondered about my faith and the Christian Church. Some of the ceremony of church services often made me think we have lost the simplicity of Jesus' message.

I also found it difficult to accept that I could never qualify as a full member of the Church simply because I was female. The Church seems to be as much of a male hierarchy as any other aspect of human society. I expected an intellectual religion to be above such discrimination. Jesus had to be male. A woman would not have been able to lead an independent life at that time. It would have been equally difficult for women to become disciples of a nomadic teacher. However, considering the social restrictions on women's lives at the time, Jesus raised the profile of women. I could see no reason, in theory, why a woman should not be able to teach and influence humanity in a philosophical field just as much as a man.

I was also critical of how the Church treated gays. Why should the fact that someone wants to share their life and have a sexual relationship with someone of the same sex make them less acceptable as a religious teacher or as a member of the Church? The only wrongs are to inflict our beliefs on others or to exploit others. Heterosexuals can be just as guilty of these transgressions. I thought everyone should be sensitive about showing their sexuality in public. We may be able to choose how we display our sexuality but we cannot choose what causes our arousal. I did not think that gender, race or orientation should affect our ability to be a moral example to others. No one chooses the circumstances of their birth.

Jesus took the basic messages behind the Jewish commandments and added a layer of sophistication. In addition to the fundamental laws, such as not stealing or murdering for example, he added the requirement that we would treat others as we would like to be treated. He changed the emphasis from being rewarded in an afterlife just because we worship God to helping others in our daily lives. In other words, it doesn't matter how good we look but only what good we do. Any human society naturally fears anyone who is different. I thought the Christian Church, as a sophisticated and thinking religion, should be above such primitive fears. We do not choose to be male or female, rich or poor, gay or heterosexual.

I had been touched by the concern that Anita and Eberhardt had taken over my welfare. They were strangers and yet they had taken me into their family without any reservations. My childhood had been spent in institutions surrounded by adults who espoused the Christian faith. It seemed that there were good and thoughtful people and others who were less so. In April 1979, I decided: *"God exists but as to religion I believe that as long as human beings love each other that is what matters. Don't think I believe in eternal life. Is it not a little childish to think that we must do good in this life otherwise we suffer later?"* A week later I wrote: *"Keep thinking God doesn't exist. Religion seems too primitive an idea."*

The concept of a God is a useful mechanism in motivating us to do the right thing (much like the drink driving laws). I hoped I could live my life as Jesus recommended without the spiritual threat.

On the evening of my eighteenth birthday, Anita and Eberhardt took me out for a meal. As they were getting ready, I stood in the hall, observing myself in the mirror. I considered what it meant to be eighteen. I had gained personal confidence by thinking through my beliefs. Until now, my life had been in the hands of others. Now that I was adult, I was responsible for my own happiness and for making something of my life. I had also matured intellectually, figuring out what I wanted for my personal development. There was no prospect of my parents keeping me. I had to make my own way in the world and at eighteen, I felt well qualified to do this.

I had seen how much I could achieve through my own efforts. I had travelled abroad, first to France and then to Germany. I had earned my own money. I naturally turned to the idea of studying and finding a professional career that would support me in life. I had vague ideas of husband and family. But talking with Anita had woken me up to the modern opportunities for women. By combining family and a career, she provided a role model. The fact that career advancement depends on the ability to make oneself popular (one way or another) never occurred to me. The fact that many men look on women just as sex objects also never occurred to me. I enjoy intellectual ideals but I am naïve about politics.

I didn't meet my first lover until end of my gap year in the summer of 1979. During this year, I masturbated more than at any other time in my life. With no man in my bed, I had complete privacy to enjoy my own responsiveness. My lifestyle was relatively relaxed and there was a novelty to the experience. My expectations for my sex life were drawn from books because no woman ever gave me a real account of sex. The fact that women do not compare notes openly and honestly was a sign that my expectations were set too high. I embarked on adult life hoping for arousal and orgasm with a lover. Later I realised that most women, having much lower expectations, are content with the reality they experience. My responsiveness meant that I was less embarrassed about sex as well as more confident of my sexual experiences than most women are.

# PART VII: POSTSCRIPT

## Finding my own way and meeting my life-partner

When I returned from Frankfurt, I decided to book a driving test. Trevor had bought a second-hand mini but it was never mine. I spent a few weeks in Dorset, driving around the countryside with Alan. We got on well together. He was easy to talk to. I think he was amazed by my adventurousness. When I told him that Sarah and I were planning to hitchhike in the South of France, he immediately lectured me on the dangers of young girls getting into cars with strangers. Alan said Marseille was particularly dangerous. I wanted to go to Nice. I listened but I had no intention of limiting my freedom on the basis of other people's fears. People often want to stop others doing what they are afraid to do themselves. I knew that we would have to be careful. My parents never commented.

Sarah and I spent ten days hitchhiking from Nice to Saint Raphael and back. One truck driver talked about topless sun-bathing. A couple of young men pointed out that we could do little to stop them driving us somewhere since there were no doors in the back. But they were friendly enough. Sarah went home and I found a job through an agency in Nice. I went to live with a family in St Jean Cap Ferrat, which is where I met my first boyfriend, David, who was a chef from Liverpool. I was impressed with David's ambitions for his career. He was keen to earn money and easy to talk to. I found him attractive and decided that I would agree to sex with him. That was when I discovered the massive cover-up over sex. I felt absolutely nothing. No erotic arousal and no physical stimulation.

Dave said my experience was typical but he still expected regular sex. I continued because I enjoyed pleasuring the man I loved. I was intent on having a career and we had no reliable contraception. It was an enormous risk to take. I can only assume that female hormones and eons of evolution have made young women ready to take risk for no reason. Men see this amenability as a female weakness and use it to insist on getting what they want. These are instinctive behaviours. The sexes have a symbiotic relationship rather than consciously exploitative. David had a temper and I was often in tears. But I gained significant personal confidence and enjoyed a feeling of emotional reassurance from having a lover.

While we were in France, David's parents came to visit. His mother created a big row one evening about the fact that David and I were sharing a bedroom. I was amazed because her son was twenty-three and I was only eighteen. David had had countless one-night stands in the bars of Liverpool as well as a number of girlfriends. His mother implied that I was a wicked woman leading her son astray. It amazes me how women can be so hypocritical. Her husband was quick to point out that they had had sex before they got married.

When I returned to the UK, I went to stay with my father. David had not used condoms reliably in France. I did not want to get pregnant so I went to the doctor. I was shocked and angry when he lectured me on the importance of morality for women. I explained that I had a boyfriend. The doctor suggested that, once I was on the pill, all that might change. Now that reliable contraception was available, I had assumed that women had the same sexual freedom as men. I didn't appreciate that originally the pill was only offered to married women. Men seem to see sexual freedom as a male right that women can never share. I wanted a prescription so I kept quiet.

Years later I went to have a coil removed by a doctor. I explained that my husband had had a vasectomy (after the birth of our third child) so that I no longer needed to worry about contraception. The doctor asked me whether I was having sex with other men. I was shocked by his question. I didn't see that my sex life was any of his business. I thought he was refusing to remove the coil. I was angry that a doctor could dictate my method of contraceptive and that I, as a mature adult, had no right to choose what happened to my body. Men escape morality lectures because they don't go to doctors for contraception. Even today society seems to accept the double standard that men can expect sexual freedom but that women should always feel constrained by responsibilities. In truth a woman is under pressure from her lover. No one acknowledges that you can't have a relationship with a man without offering sex.

David came to stay with me for a couple of days in Dorset. Before his visit, Alan suggested to me privately that we should sleep in separate bedrooms so as not to offend my father. Trevor, always the coward, was not brave enough to face me himself. I was amazed. Trevor with all his brazen promiscuity and obvious sex drive, was disapproving of sex before marriage. I told Alan that it was unthinkable for me to sleep in a separate bedroom from the man I had been living with in France. I had grown up with two promiscuous parents, who I assumed espoused modern views on sexuality. Trevor never talked to me. He never even checked that I was using contraception. I didn't tell him about the doctor's visit.

I thought it ironic that my father, a homosexual, who had spent his life enjoying his sexuality to the full, should lecture his daughter on morality. I had already noted men and women's different levels of interest in sex. These behaviours were also reflected in general fiction and movies for general release. It was only in erotic fiction that the contradiction occurred. This probably explains why my father enjoyed stories of sexual women but in reality, he wanted to protect his daughter from men. He accepted that marriage in particular was a social choice based on the lifestyle a woman hoped for. The women in his family had not had career opportunities.

Trevor was hopeful that we would marry men from his own family's class but I was more realistic. Although we had had an upper-class privileged education, we lacked the family connections that would place us in that social class. I wanted a partner who would accept my independent personality and my unconventional family background. Trevor felt duty-bound to guide us but he was not confident about how to do this. When he did interfere, he would frequently offer advice in an imperious and domineering manner. He wrote to me when I was nineteen: *"You have caused me so few worries and anxieties and for this I am so grateful to you. I do not feel much satisfaction with my puny and miserable efforts with my own life. But I do feel very proud of you and perhaps I may be allowed to feel that I had something to do with helping you to grow up as you have despite so many adverse conditions."* (26.12.80)

David and I lived together while I was at University. Trevor complained that I was a common law wife when I should be concentrating on my studies. Again, it was typical of my father to have such out-dated views. His attitudes came straight from his

Edwardian parents who he had tried so hard to escape himself. I'm sure he wouldn't have said the same thing if I was a man. The tradition is that a woman has the status of her husband. If she is not married then she has no social status. But times were changing. Or supposed to be. Many young people live together but cover up and lie to their parents about it. I was not willing to lie when my parents had been so promiscuous. Dave and I split up after two years. My parents made no comment. Their disinterest was typical of my relationship with them. They never seemed to engage on my life.

A year later I met my future husband, Peter, in Nantes in France. We were both employed for the summer holiday after university to do programming work for a microchip manufacturer. We quickly fell in love and lived together back in the UK. On our return, I started my 3 years of accountancy training and Peter studied for his doctorate. We married in June 1984 when we were both twenty-three. I thought that Peter would make an intelligent and loving companion and, should we decide later to have children, a good father. Peter and I were both on student salaries, so for our honeymoon we went camping with the car and a tent for three weeks. I enjoyed showing Peter France, Switzerland, Germany and Italy. We also went to stay with Anita and Eberhardt in Frankfurt.

Peter had grown up the middle child in a family of five. Peter's father, Rex Thomas, had a strong belief in the value of family, being himself the seventh child in a family of eight. He had grown up in a new council house in the pretty Wiltshire village of Lydiard Millicent. His father had a job with The Great Western Railway at Swindon. Rex was able at school but more enthusiastic about playing cricket. He left school at fifteen to start work as a junior clerk for The Great Western Railway. Peter's mother, Kathleen Tommey, grew up with similar levels of poverty. There was never any encouragement for doing homework and Kath had to help her mother in the house from a young age. On leaving school, Kath went into domestic service and worked in a sewing factory. Rex and Kath married in April 1953 both in their early twenties. To better support his growing family, Rex studied to become a Company Accountant in evening classes. Most of his career was spent at the Avon Rubber Company in Melksham where the family settled.

They had a traditional marriage. Rex built his career and played cricket in his free time. Kath cooked, cleaned and raised their five children. Peter and his younger brother were needed to help Rex on the family allotment in the summer. The girls helped their mother in the house but even Peter learned how to bake bread and could cook a roast dinner. Kath made most of the children's clothes herself as well as taking on additional piecework, sewing and knitting for low wages. Kath's own childhood was tough and she ruled her children with strict discipline. Peter escaped the constant chores by spending much of his time listening to music in his room.

Rex invested in a camper van and the family holidays were spent in the New Forest or on the South Coast. Peter's academic ability became apparent during his teenage years at the local state school, George Ward. Peter was practical as well as academically able. As a teenager, he earned money mending televisions and decorating neighbours' houses. He learned car mechanics from his father and taught himself electronics through various practical projects. His teachers wanted him to go to Cambridge but Peter preferred the course that was offered by Southampton University. He was awarded a first-class honours degree in Electronic Engineering.

We both worked hard at our careers over the years and tried to optimize our income. I qualified as a Chartered Accountant and Peter obtained his PhD in Electronic Engineering. We started out with £1,000 from my mother which we used as a house deposit. We also received £700 from Peter's parents, which we spent on furniture. I was interested in property and Peter was keen to use his practical skills to save us money. We worked together to invest strategically in the properties we owned to gradually increase our capital. Even later when we had children, we worked full time and restored a derelict property so that we could optimise the money we had. We employed nannies and au pairs to help us in the week. At weekends we went ice skating (in winter) and horse riding (in summer) as a family. Family holidays were either skiing or sailing.

## My father's illness and his ever-reducing capital

As Sarah and I were embarking on adult life, my father's capital was disappearing fast. Offering bed and breakfast never made money.

Trevor decided to sell the cottage in Zeals and rent a flat in London. He could no longer afford to buy in London and wanted to be able to live off his capital. He and Alan moved into a tiny top floor flat in Notting Hill Gate over a shabby terrace of businesses. The entrance was next door to a launderette. The flat was not as respectable as the properties Trevor had owned previously. But he never mentioned this and seemed pleased just to be back in central London. Trevor was used to creating a home and he quickly made it feel cosy. The paintwork was old, the electrics too frightening to contemplate and the window frames stained with grime deposited from London's polluted air. Traffic roared past all day and most of the night. On the positive side, there was always a shop open in the street below and he was only five minutes from the tube station.

On one of my visits I found a magazine under his coffee table. It was full of naked men, in various poses, displaying their non-erect penises. I found some of them very attractive but I noted that the visual images did not arouse me. My arousal seemed to rely on some kind of story and narrative description of the feelings of the participants. Obviously, this was very different to male arousal. I have never in my whole life had a conversation with a woman about similar experiences. Most women avoid the topic. Those who project a confident bravado, talk about pornography as if women respond sexually just as men do. So I doubt that they know what an orgasm is. The two psychological approaches are quite different.

Then in the summer of 1982 towards the end of my university days, Trevor was taken critically ill out in Kota Bahru, Malaysia. He was petrified of dying out there in a third world hospital with flies buzzing around him. As soon as he was able, Trevor wrote: *"This hospital is very much early British Empire. My cell is very basic indeed – a door to the rest of the ward and a door out onto the toilet and street!! Constant traffic noises! No windows, just open top of the walls to allow free airflow and fan. Of course, nights are awful with the heat and mosquitoes. Occasionally a bat gets in by mistake and bounces around the walls. Somehow, one just ignores it as there is little I can do about it anyway....*

*George has been amazing undertaking all the cost and buying the village store to try to find something I could taste and eat. The food is utter hell and almost indescribable. I fear I have a debt to him I can never repay. This is one time when I omitted to pick up an insurance form on departure from London Airport. Really how stupid can I be? Fortunately, he has a large amount of leave accumulated and due, so had no problems staying here an extra two weeks. But he seems to enjoy spending his money all the more if it is to help someone else." (8.6.82)*

As Trevor's condition stabilised, George moved him to a private hospital in Singapore. While he was convalescing in Singapore, I wrote to tell Trevor that I had passed my Mathematics degree with honours and been awarded an Upper Second. He replied: *"My Dear Jane, Congratulations, I was so thrilled to hear of your success. I could not be more excited or more proud of your achievements.... Myself as you see back in George's flat yesterday and getting a little stronger each day. It's exactly five weeks today it all started and now I would really like to get home...*

*I managed to pay for the first 2 ½ weeks in Kota Bahru hospital with the £600 I had put in George's account before arriving. But this last two weeks in a first-class deluxe hospital I fear will be four times that amount. If only I had had the sense to take out one of those BA insurance things on departure. Well that seems to be the story of my life: if only, this or that... Both Mother and Barbara have offered help. George says he is 'not desperate for the money at the moment'. He really is some cousin! ... All my love, please take care, Dad" (25.6.82)*

I did not usually correspond with Alan. We picked up from where we had left off effortlessly whenever we met. He usually got my news from Trevor. Alan had always lacked personal confidence. He had given up working because he found it too stressful. Now he resumed his career as a quantity surveyor. My sense of intimacy with Alan had ended when they moved to London. It transpired that Alan's drinking problem came to light while they were living in Zeals. In London, he joined the AA (Alcoholics Anonymous). I found him to be quite a different person sober and much less easy to talk to. Alan wrote to me soon after Trevor's return from Singapore, when I had just set off for France again on holiday work.

*"Dear Jane, Thanks for your letter. I hope you're enjoying your nomadic life over there. Your father arrived last Saturday. I was pleasantly surprised to see that he looked so well. He was a bit pale and thinner than before but not drastically so. He also seemed to be very jolly, which was more than I was as I had a flat tyre on the way to meet him. (Spent 15 minutes looking in the boot for the spare only to realise it was under the bonnet!) I also got a parking ticket as I was carrying the bags upstairs having left the car at the door. Your father left for Durham on the Tuesday. I've spoken to him several times since and he sounds very well indeed. I haven't been doing anything very exciting – just trudging along. Today I lay in Kensington Gardens listening to the brass band. So now I am a shocking pink colour and a bit painful. Yesterday I did the battle of Harrods sale. I hope all is well in France. Looking forward to hearing from you soon. Lots of Love, Alan" (10.7.82)*

Later Alan moved out of the Notting Hill Gate flat to live a life of his own. He seemed to be living a trendy life with his new job and new friends. Trevor had invested a small amount of his capital in a property out in Sydney, Australia together with his friend Jack. Trevor acquired a new flatmate, called John, who seemed a most unlikely companion for my father. He was a much younger and very tall Australian. John never made any conversation so I never knew him. Following his illness in the Far East, Trevor was diagnosed with colon cancer and in December 1984, he was taken into St Steven's hospital, Chelsea to have a colostomy operation.

*"My Dear Jane, At last some of the strings and tubes have been severed and my hands are more free. The stitches are out and some progress is now apparent.... I must thank you for your nice letters and the time you take to write to me. I have had so many nice good wishes and prayers: from a week of masses from the 1st floor Catholic ladies at 151 (neighbours at Notting Hill Gate) to rather less religious prayers from my two camp charlies in San Francisco and an offer to go there for what they call R&R (rest and recuperation). George sent masses of roses from Singapore and Dr Chris flowers from K.L....*

*I do get awful bouts of depression – emotions seemed to be on a knife-edge of deep depression and extreme hilarity. Have had lots* of laughs. But it's so easy to cry and feel sorry for oneself. I think it's a lot to do with years of no real love and affection in one's life and when under stress no one to hold or touch. So, that when one comes face to face with some real kindness, it's hard to control oneself. After one such deep mood, I now have visits from so many lovely girls. One wonders where they all come from. Some of them newly from training at the Westminster hospital and quite lost in a new world. Have a lot of thinking to do and begin to feel I should eventually move up to be near to Barbara... Lots of love" (13.12.84)

Despite his operation and his regular prescription for colostomy bags, Trevor continued to travel. Travel was his lifeline, providing the companionship and sexual fun that he could no longer afford in London. With money becoming increasingly precious, he stayed with friends. He went to Sydney to see Jack, San Francisco to visit the camp charlies of the above letter and to George in Singapore and Chris in Kuala Lumpur. I noted that these destinations all offered some degree of gay tolerance. George wrote: *"Thank you for your long and chatty letter way back. Now we are in the throes of your Pa's illness. I have talked to John, Barbara and Derry in Edinburgh. I think he will be going to Chester-le-Street. John will return to Australia. In time, Trevor will get used to this thing of his in some horrible way but he will adapt. He did have the thing before in Kota Bahru until we got rid of it. He was quite adept at managing himself. Of course, a lot of the fun in life he used to have, here and there, will be gone. I talked to the surgeon who did him and he didn't think the future looked too rosy...."* (11.12.84)

Trevor's little flat in Notting Hill Gate was convenient. I was not a frequent visitor but sometimes I would ask to sleep on his sofa bed in the lounge. We kept in touch by phone. Trevor wrote: *"My dear Jane, Enjoyed your visit last night so very much. It's super talking to you and thank you for the bottle of bubbly. Even though battered and bruised and almost completely impotent, I should think myself lucky to be alive. Spared for a few more years, I hope! ... Anyway, my love to you both, Trevor"* (15.2.85)

Towards the end of 1985, as his declining health and his future dependency on others dawned, Trevor moved to Framwellgate Moor, Durham to be close to his sister Barbara. I was surprised by this return North after all these years. But family ties are strong at the end of life. He bought a former pit cottage, a terraced house with a tiny garden in which he planted roses, always a favourite of his. Barbara employed a local couple who now supported Trevor as well. Even when he admitted to being incapable, Trevor continued to lust after young men. Travelling gave him the sexual variety and freedom he craved. He needed love as much as sex.

"Dear Jane and Peter, Went shopping in a K.L. market with Ipoh, Chris's housekeeper. She only comes up to my titties but with her in front and the driver behind was quite sensational. The place smelt like an unflushed public toilet but exotic, nevertheless. One shot was an instant execution of chickens: chopped, plucked and corpsed before they were even cold. How I wish I had explored this part of the world more thoroughly when I was younger. Even wish I could adopt one just to cuddle in the lonely nights. Still feel that I have been completely neutered. Chaste and untouched by human hands. Maybe Bangkok will be therapeutic! Lots of love to you both from your wandering aged Daddy – so glad you have someone to love!" (9.5.86)

I visited Trevor a couple of months before his death. He was much his normal self despite being on strong painkillers. He was still driving and in reasonable spirits having survived a second, long northern winter: *"Dear Jane, the winter seems to go on and on forever. It's been the longest, loneliest one I have ever known. I am tired of moaning but what else? My taste for life has gone but, worst of all, my taste for food has gone... Looking back I don't think I have ever been really alone, without anyone to communicate with. Even if I had the 'get up and go' to go out and seek some company, there is not a great deal of intellect in Framwellgate Moor.... Love, Dad"* (29.3.87)

One Saturday in July 1987, I picked up the phone. Trevor had been admitted to hospital. He was incoherent but his confusion was obvious. He didn't understand what had happened. I imagined him alone in the hospital with no one beside him. Peter and I drove up North and went straight to the hospital. Trevor was unconscious and I can only hope that he knew I was there. I left him overnight and then felt terrible the next day when they told me that a nurse always sits with dying patients through the night. I sat by him the next day and he died at around 4pm. It took some hours for his death to sink in. I cried as much from regret as sadness. I regretted that my parents had not wanted to know me better as an adult.

Peter and I had booked a holiday in the Far East later that summer. I wanted to show Peter the exotic sights that I had seen when I was eleven. While we were staying with George in Singapore, I received a letter from Trevor's friend Jack. *"Dear Jane, Please accept my sincerest sympathy. Your father was a great pal and we were writing often this year, knowing that it possibly was the last. I went to see him prior to leaving the UK to live here. He and Barbara took me out and I dined with Alastair, Barbara and Trevor. He was very much with it and given his early medical training was pretty au-fait with his illness... He was very confident that his daughters would do well where he felt he had failed but that failure was only a view of life he learned from others as his other actions more than made up for it.... Yours Jack"* (18.7.87)

Just a few years after my father's death, Barbara called me with the news that Alan had died. I had been unaware of his illness and I was shocked by his death because he was so young. I assume that it may have been HIV related. My father was very lucky not to get AIDS himself. I never knew whether the cancer was related.

## My mother's business and her drinking habit

As Sarah and I were growing up, Jo was starting to wonder what she might do with the rest of her life. She was frustrated with always being poor. She disliked the associated sense of social inferiority. Her younger brother Tommy had followed Arthur into the fish and chip trade. Now Tommy had a shop in Reading to sell. He was also willing to give Jo an interest free loan. This made the venture possible because she wouldn't have qualified for a bank loan. The shop was on the Basingstoke Road, in Reading. It had a prominent position on a busy road, which meant a good level of trade.

Simon moved to a new school in Reading. He and Jo lived over the shop for a couple of years before she earned enough money for a mortgage on a house. Now that she had money, Jo became a habitual drinker. She believed that because she could stop drinking (because of a lack of money) this proved she was not addicted. But if alcoholism is defined as being out of control then she certainly was. Jo related stories of her drunken escapades to everyone. She often had no memory of how she got home. Once she ended up in a ditch, which she laughed about. I thought Simon was old enough to refuse to get into the car. But she also drove Anne when she was drunk, which I thought was wrong. When I suggested she should go to Alcoholics Anonymous, Jo told me I was high and mighty.

Once she had the shop Jo talked about nothing but the fish and chip trade. Sarah's and my schooling had already separated us from her but once we were adults with our own partners there was an even greater divide. She rarely came to visit. So I usually visited her, which was difficult because the bed linen was not always clean and we often had to wipe plates and glasses before using them. I could not help but find it ironic that she was so disinterested in us as adults. She had devoted so much effort and suffered such heartache in fighting for custody of us as children. Jo appeared to be financially successful in Reading. She went on luxury holidays and after a few years, moved to a large thatched cottage in the country.

After a few years, Jo decided that the Reading shop was too much work. Once again, she turned to Tommy for help and arranged an exchange with another of Tommy's shops on the coast in Poole. She had always wanted to live by the sea. The new business was seasonal and much smaller than the Reading shop. Initially Jo and Simon lived in the flat over the shop. Later she bought a house nearby. She had little time to keep her house clean and, with her drinking continuing out of control, she started having sex with men on a casual basis. She told me how some mornings when she woke up, she would be surprised to find a strange man lying next to her.

Jo worked until she dropped and then went somewhere hot and cheap, usually Tunisia, for a holiday. She met a young man out there who was happy to have sex with an older woman. She knew him over many years as she returned to Tunisia regularly. One day, Jo found out that this man had invited his friends for a gang bang. Luckily, she got away. I never knew what she expected me to say to these confidences. Was I supposed to be shocked? She was apparently unconcerned about the dangers. I thought it ironic that if I had behaved that way, a normal parent would be outraged by such irresponsible behaviour. But what does one say to a parent?

The shop in Poole never did well and the rent was high. With the economic depression of the early 1990s, the British stopped going to the seaside even in the summer. She wrote: *"The last two months I have been working seven days and six nights until I could not work any longer. I had to close the shop for three days to have a rest...."* She drank German hock to cope with her exhaustion and it was rare to speak to her sober. I tried to persuade her to get out while she could but she remained convinced that she could work her way out of her problems. I used to dread her calling and each call ended with my frustration that I could do nothing to help.

In the end, she left it too late and went bankrupt. There was a problem with the lease on the flat, for which there was no planning permission. Jo blamed the lawyers who had acted for her on the original conveyancing. Arthur offered to pay for his own lawyer, to review the evidence and to advise Jo on what action she could take. I could not see how Jo could lose out. The advice was free and she did not have to take it if she did not want to. I was exasperated when Jo wrote to me to turn down the offer. I replied saying that I thought she was being stupid. I was intentionally blunt. I wanted either to push her into action or, more likely, put an end to the frustration of listening to her endless problems. Predictably, Jo was offended by my letter and I did not hear from her for many years afterwards.

Having been obsessive about the fish and chip trade, Jo now became obsessed with the injustice that she had suffered at the hands of her solicitors. She set about attempting to sue them for the loss of her business and her house. Her campaign often involved illegal activities. Once she was arrested by the police for painting graffiti on the public offices in Poole. She also used to beg on the street. From then on, I heard from her sporadically, usually because she needed some favour. After a break of five years, Jo asked to stay with me for a Saturday night in August 1996. We talked about my children and her memories of our childhood. She left the next day and I did not see her again for another eight years.

Most of the time Jo seemed just like anyone else. I concluded that mental illness means someone behaves in ways that cannot be explained or understood by others. I continued to receive occasional correspondence that I dreaded opening. One mailing was a flyer she sent to everyone she knew. It was an open letter to Gerry Adams whom she claimed to have personally met in Belfast, and was supposedly copied to the American media, British media, Bill Clinton and Tony Blair. Finally, I heard that she was being held in Gloucester prison because she had failed to appear for a court hearing of her suspected arson attempt on the solicitor's offices.

Arthur visited her and reported back that she seemed comfortable. She had meals and books from the library. Arthur agreed to bail her out. He also gave her money, which she spent on a luxury holiday in Mauritius. However, she then initiated a hate campaign against him because she believed he had a letter she needed for her trial. One postcard she sent to Arthur had to be placed in an envelope by the postal service because it was too obscene to go through the general mail. She also put up defamatory posters in the pubs near where my uncle lived accusing him of various crimes. Personally, I was relieved not to be involved in my mother's life.

In November 2000 I received a letter from a psychiatric hospital in Poole, telling me that they were holding my mother under powers in Section 48 and 49 of the Mental Health Act 1983. She had been transferred from prison. Jo, having lost contact with Sarah, had named me as her next of kin. I considered whether I was right to remain distant from my mother. If she was not responsible for her own actions did that increase my obligation to try to do something to help? The hospital told me that adults are deemed responsible for themselves. If not, the state takes over. My dilemma was solved when Jo was released from hospital a few weeks later and moved back to prison still awaiting trial. Jo had produced evidence that convinced the appeal hearing that she was not suffering from paranoia as they had thought. Her evidence included a statement from a psychiatrist (dated May 1997): *"I think it is very difficult to see the truth of this situation... but from the medical point of view, this patient is not suffering from any psychiatric illness."*

Next Jo asked various friends to approach me for money. Richard was a longer-term friend and lover of Jo's. He called me on the day of my fortieth birthday. I asked him if he knew all the facts of Jo's situation and it became clear that she had not told him everything. He told me that he had just had Jo to stay with him. He had paid her bail and I was aghast when he told me it was £10,000. I was amazed that Jo expected people to pay such a large sum of money on her behalf. He said that during her stay, Jo had become verbally abusive to him and so he had taken her back to prison. He had realised that she had no intention of returning voluntarily regardless of the large sum that he had put up for her. In January 2002, Jo was tried and sentenced to 2 years in prison. As she had served most of her sentence by then, she was released to continue her crusade.

I used to feel sorry for Jo that she had her children taken away. Later I wondered why she left Trevor. It was not as if she had another man in her life. Jo was an emotionally disturbed young woman who fell in love with a gay man nearly 20 years older than herself. She was looking for someone to admire and, of course, someone to love her. Self-evidently any man of that age is likely to have had other relationships. He is likely to revert to his former love life. Jo could not stay when her husband evidently did not love her. Later Jo acknowledged that if she had realised that she would lose her home and custody of her children, she might never have left. It was not entirely clear why she handed us over to Trevor in Battersea. Most mothers look after their children no matter what the obstacles. She seemed to find the responsibility too demanding.

## The split with Sarah and reconciling personalities

Sarah had come through school in my academic shadow. The schools had always been ready to praise me but they were much less complimentary about Sarah. In the end, Sarah's O level results were equal to mine and her A levels were considerably better. Evidently, we should never be discouraged by the system. Once we left school, our lives took different directions. At college Sarah made friends with a girl called Caroline. Once Jo moved to Reading, Caroline's middle-class parents became Sarah's surrogate family. After a gap year, Sarah went to Bath University to study

Architecture. I was hurt that she did not keep in touch with me. She moved often and I always had to get her new address from Jo.

Trevor had said that for many years in his youth he rarely went home. Likewise, Sarah was more successful at creating a wider circle of friends than I had ever been. Despite the obvious signs that Sarah already had the relationships she valued in her life, I continued to try to meet up with her. Each time I would be offended by her behaviour. She either failed to show or brought a friend along so that she did not have to talk to me alone. The final straw came when Sarah invited me to her twenty-first birthday party.

I was living in Southampton. Peter and I drove up to Bath after work on a Friday evening for her party at 10.30pm. After a long working week, I was not keen on arriving so late but Sarah insisted that she wanted me there. This was a key misunderstanding between us. Sarah simply wanted to have me somewhere in the background at her party. Whereas I had assumed that she would want to spend some time together to justify my investment of time and effort. We waited half an hour for her and then we left. The next day Sarah phoned in all innocence to ask why I had not come.

I explained that this was the final humiliation in a long history of her ignoring me and standing me up. I needed her to demonstrate that she wanted to have contact with me. Sarah thought that all she had to do was put on a superficially friendly act whenever she chanced to see me. I have not found a way to stop people taking advantage of my generous nature. I accept it is my own weakness but I steer clear of people who only give when they want something.

After our call, Sarah evidently spoke to Trevor because I received a long and critical letter from him. He had only heard Sarah's side of the story and immediately assumed that I was in the wrong. I was disappointed because I thought we had a good relationship and that he knew that I am not usually unreasonable. To avoid conflict, he wrote a letter rather than talk to me directly. I could not understand why Sarah was so upset. So far, I was only one making effort. I did not think it a crime to ask her to make some effort once in a while.

I need to share my thoughts to feel close to someone I love. Sarah had made it clear that our relationship was unimportant to her. My pride was hurt and I felt rejected. I thought that it was important to invest in relationships. When everything was going well, Sarah never gave a thought to family. But when she had problems, she thought that family should naturally provide support and sympathy.

Sarah assumed that I disapproved of her because I did things differently. She wanted to live for now, spend too much and then hope someone else would pay. I lacked confidence that anyone would pay my bills. I did not like to ask my parents for anything because I did not want to test the love, I hoped they returned. I was proud of being able to look after myself. My parents were not terribly interested in my problems. Perhaps no one is. I learned that if I had a problem then I had to deal with it by myself. I always thought that I could use my abilities to help those around me. I have come to realise that most people don't want to change their behaviour or the way they are. They assume their problems are an unavoidable consequence of life. They don't want to be helped.

If you try to help, they feel judged and criticised. When I was a teenager Jo told me that I lacked compassion. I never understood what she meant. If something goes wrong in my life, I analyse what happened and change my approach to avoid the same problem in future. I save money or make do, where Sarah continues spending. I assumed that adults accept the consequences of the choices they make. I didn't appreciate that I am very disciplined. My ability to be dispassionate about the choices I make, makes me unusual. My weakness is never learning to take a less ambitious route and not understanding that other people do not see things the same way.

From Sarah's perspective, I was the one who had caused the rift. She explained later that she had been taken unawares by my anger. She heard that I thought she was selfish and irresponsible and that I never wanted to see her again. Sarah wanted to defend her position and so she wrote five long sides to explain:

*"Dear Jane, Since our phone call I have thought a lot, cried a lot and really looked at myself to find justification for the things I am being accused of. I feel that you have not been fair on me, mainly because you know little about me, except what you hear from Jo, which I know is largely my fault. When you came back with Dave,*

*bought a house together, spent every minute of your time with him, the odd weekend you might come home but it was always with Dave. I found we began to gradually lose touch with each other.*

*It's very difficult to carry on really knowing someone when the only time you see them, they're with someone else who needs all that person's attention most of the time. I don't call that discarding your friendship. I made friends who had time for me, who knew me. I think this is where our paths diverged. You got involved with a boyfriend I got involved with close friends. I'm really sorry I wasn't there at 10.30pm. I think you have every reason to be annoyed with me especially after the last time but understand me for a second. When I asked you, I said you might not see much of me since lots of people were coming but I thought you might enjoy it....*

*You're so disapproving of the way I spend money, what I do, my values etc... I could only see you looking at me saying 'You've brought it all on to yourself, Sarah'. I'm afraid I couldn't take that. I know for myself that I have made an awful lot of mistakes over the past year and have taken the toll for them. The thing I need most at the moment is sympathy, love and understanding. But Jane you judge me the whole time. I have never lived up to your expectations. I don't think I ever will. We do things differently.... Bye, take care, Sarah" (19.2.84)*

In many families, even with divorced parents, usually at least one parent's home creates a family forum for keeping in touch. We lacked the social glue that married parents often provide in bringing the family together. In other families, brothers and sisters might be happy to live quite separate lives, only meeting occasionally through duty or habit. I had grown up with Sarah under difficult family circumstances and I thought our relationship was different. Sarah was popular and had plenty of friends. I did not have the same close friendships so I was more reliant on my family relationships.

Sarah married a German called Thomas, a fellow architect and they moved out to Berlin. Unfortunately, the strains of working together meant that the marriage did not last. Sarah returned to live in London, working part-time either for private clients or teaching architectural studies. When she was 44, Sarah had a baby girl with her Australian partner, Russell. We saw each other occasionally. Given Jo's behaviour, I thought that I had done well not to refuse all contact with Sarah. Forgiveness does not mean condoning what has happened but rather accepting that everyone is different.

## Jo's children and the irony of illegitimacy

For many years, it looked as if Simon would be set up with capital and a good income for life. Jo had always said that she intended leaving all her money and her business to Simon. She believed that Sarah and I didn't need money as we had the benefit of a private education. Jo had wanted Simon to learn to run the shop. They worked together for a while but it's never easy working for a parent. Simon decided to enter more regular employment. He got a job as an insurance clerk where he met Denys. Later when they married, Simon and Denys bought their own house. It came at a desperate time for Jo and she was hurt by what she saw as his desertion.

Jo had set up an endowment policy for Simon's benefit. She contributed for 10 years but when she could no longer afford the payments, she told Simon he would have to make them for the last three years. When the policy matured, it was not a large sum and Simon used the money as a deposit on his first house. Jo was in dire financial straits at the time and she felt that Simon should have given her the money. While Simon and Denys were planning their wedding, Jo called to say that she would not be attending because Simon had included his uncles in the guest list. Jo was offended that Simon would invite Tommy who she believed had caused her business troubles. She told Simon she never wanted to see him again. Fortunately, Simon's parents-in-law provided some of the moral and practical support that was missing from his own family.

Simon wrote: *"Life at Kingsclere was without doubt a very stable, family orientated environment, where Mum was very loving and caring of us. Although without money, I felt that I had everything I ever had wanted in terms of material things. The only thing I wanted was a Dad. I don't remember Mum's tiredness. However, I don't doubt this for one minute. She clearly worked hard and I was too young to remember. Reading was different. It just proves, in Mum's case, that money doesn't bring happiness. Her newfound* wealth meant she could drink when she liked, which seemed to be whenever she wasn't working...

Your acknowledgement of my problems accepting illegitimacy were appreciated. You are correct in assuming that I have always had problems living with this big dark cloud over my head and until now have never dared to talk about it outside my marriage. I have always been faced with the dilemma of how to react when asked about my father. I feel very bitter having never had a male figure to look up to, especially in my younger years. I am convinced that this has greatly affected the way I have turned out and my obvious lack of confidence and shyness. I have very little knowledge of my real father, Barney, so it was good to hear your account of him coming to visit us at Kingsclere. Strangely, I have no desire to find him after all these years."

Anne continued to live with Mrs Peters who lived her life around her, going shopping with her, taking an interest in her hobbies and going on holiday with her. Anne's pastimes often focused on television personalities and she followed the lives of various actors and sportsmen. Simon and his wife Denys were both excellent with Anne and they maintained regular phone contact. Mrs Peters and her husband spent their lives dedicated to caring for the mentally handicapped. They had even organised charity fund-raising to provide a local day centre. Later Mrs Peters planned ahead for her own old age. Anne went to live in a nearby home for the mentally handicapped with regular weekend visits to Mrs Peters. Given her parents, Anne was lucky to have had such a caring foster mother.

Jo had told me many tales from her past as I was growing up and I always wondered whether the story about her adopted baby was true. In the spring of 2001, my uncle Arthur called to say that Stephanie had contacted him. Stephanie wanted to meet her mother. As I picked up the phone to call her, I wondered whether there was a gentle way of breaking the news that Jo was currently in Gloucester prison. Stephanie and I arranged to meet in Cardiff. We spent four hours catching up on family history. Stephanie had grown up as a single child of an older couple. They had told her when she was ten that she was adopted. Her foster mother was disappointed when Stephanie turned out to be such a tomboy.

Stephanie married young and had three children but the marriage was not a happy one. Her husband buried himself in work and interacted little with the family. Following a disastrous move to the Channel Islands, Stephanie decided it was time for a new life for herself and her children. She came to accept what she had known for some time; that she was lesbian. Stephanie met an older woman who became her partner and parent to her children. Despite being rejected by their local church for being gay, Stephanie and Pam were happy with their Christian faith and family life together.

Stephanie explained that her faith centred on her relationship with God. For her, being Christian involves more than simply applying a moral code to life. She believed that sin is not about breaking the moral code but about a lack of relationship with God. She considered attendance at church to be only the outward indication of a person's relationship with God. Stephanie had found an emotional approach to faith whereas I had approached Christianity from a moral perspective. I recognised that in more difficult times we are all inclined to turn to God for spiritual support. I can see the benefits of virtues such as tolerance and forgiveness. But I enjoyed the moral lessons and I had a more intellectual sense of connection with God. We should always answer to our conscience and, in that sense, God is always with us. I appreciated the following wisdom from The Lyttelton Hart-Davis Letters (1956):

*"Clearly one can go only a certain distance by intellectual ways – the final step must surely be an act of faith."*

My interest in cosmology led me to question the nature of God. We now know that, relative to the rest of the universe, our sun is like a grain of sand on a beach. Not only is humanity insignificant in terms of the vastness of space, we are also a minor blip in terms of time. Our current estimate for the Big Bang, the beginning of time, is that it occurred more than 13 billion years ago. To make sense of the strings of zeros involved, the current age of the universe can be compared with a calendar year. If the Big Bang, that created the universe, happened on January $1^{st}$ (13.7 billion years ago) then the Earth, together with the solar system, was formed on September 1st (4.6 billion years ago). Mammals appeared on December 27th

(200 million years ago) and homo sapiens finally appeared at ten minutes to midnight on December 31st (just 200,000 years ago).

The Bible refers to God as if he were a person. But few people think of God as existing in terms of flesh and blood. Compared with the God of the Old Testament, the picture of God that Jesus gave us was more compassionate, more approachable and perhaps more human. At the time of my confirmation my interpretation of the Christian God was that, although he was invisible, he did have a spiritual presence. As a teenager, I had envisaged God as a superior being who would judge my behaviour and motives dispassionately. I could not lie to him because he was always present and all knowing. My understanding is that Christians believe in the existence of an entity, separate from ourselves that is stronger and better than we are. Later I lost faith in such an entity.

Many aspects of science seem fantastic to us but perhaps the most perplexing is the concept of our own consciousness. Regardless of how scientists explain the physical world, we experience more than the atoms and forces described in physics. Our brains may operate on chemical and electrical signals but this does not fully describe our awareness of the world around us. Everything in religion deals with the human condition. God is not a concept that relates to other life forms, either on Earth or elsewhere, but only to human beings. Without human beings, the concept of a God has no meaning. People often ask whether God exists but this is a meaningless question. A spiritual god is conceptual by nature. We can be sure that the concept exists because it was conceived by humans. God is a concept that people use to motivate and uplift them in their lives.

Why does any of this matter? Firstly, in this book I wanted to describe my experience of growing up and maturing into an adult. As I entered adult life, I thought it vital to consider philosophical questions such as "Why am I here?" and "What does it all mean?" Secondly, I wanted to reconcile what I considered to be the middle-class social attitudes of the Church of England with the more fundamental moral principles I understood from the Bible. Thirdly, given my experiences in growing up, I needed to find a personal philosophy for my life that I considered moral and just. Contemplation of ideas such as these have always filled my head.

I could see that, for many people brought up within a more typical family, it might be possible to adopt a black-and-white view of society, for example, that sexual promiscuity is wrong. My dilemma was that I loved my parents but they had not lived their lives in a moral way. Between them, they had probably broken every sexual rule in the book. Although I could see that they had been selfish and inconsiderate of others, I could not agree that these sins in themselves automatically made them bad people. I hoped to apply Christian morality to my life with my own conscience as my guide.

Given that a belief in God is the keystone of Christianity, I accepted that I could not be a Christian. Although I regretted my conclusion, I appreciated the intellectual flexibility. The Church sometimes seems handicapped by tradition and history. I felt empowered to use my own judgement rather than being bound by the limitations of the establishment. I thought that we should combine the best ideas from all the world's religions and build a modern human philosophy based on moral behaviour independent of our spiritual beliefs. I decided to make up my own mind, based on my experience of human nature, as to how I would try to show consideration towards others. It is perhaps irrelevant to ask whether we believe in God. There is a force for good in each of us just as there is a force for evil within each of us, whether this is intentional or arises simply from thoughtlessness. My personal belief is that God exists as long as we are motivated to do what is good and right.

Timothy Ferris (writer on cosmology and author of 'The Whole Shebang') expresses this sentiment:

*For God's hand may be a human hand, if you reach out in loving kindness, and God's voice your voice if you but speak the truth."*

## My quest to apply scientific principles to sexuality

I hope my websites: Nosper.com, WaysWomenOrgasm.org and LearnAboutSexuality.org indicate my interest in promoting ways for men and women to live together in harmony by understanding each other's very different emotional needs. Nosper is an anagram of the word PERSON. It is deliberate that Nospers are identical and that the item distinguishing them as male or female is trivial. The addition of the ribbon or bow-tie changes how we view their capabilities. The point being that gender influences our lives, sometimes for biological reasons, other times for cultural reasons.

As a young woman, I had the impression that men and women were the same. Initially the differences are subtle but they become more apparent as we grow older. It's possible that we become more vocal about expressing our views over time and more confident in behaving as we are naturally inclined to do. Understanding these fundamental differences in men and women's emotional needs can help couples in long-term relationships. We feel loved when we receive what we need emotionally. But loving someone is not about satisfying our own needs. We need to give a lover what they need.

Men often enjoy more solitary pursuits and they see their own personal success as core to how others value them. For men, intimacy revolves around their sex life with a lover. Men hope a partner will contribute enthusiastically to their intimate time together: sharing fantasies, adventurous sex play and affection. Women often enjoy more companionable pursuits and they value their relationships as an essential part of their lives. For women, intimacy involves affectionate companionship. Women hope a partner will contribute enthusiastically to their intimate time together: sharing a sense of humour, conversation and affection.

Men and women cooperate together over marriage and family. But many women dislike any discussion involving references to genital activity outside lovemaking. It is difficult for women to appreciate what sexual pleasure means to men. Sex should be discussed as much as any other topic that is vital to human emotional happiness. We need to learn how the opposite sex experiences intimacy and how men and women's very different emotional needs are satisfied.

I read a great deal as I was growing up and books often portray ideals rather than reality. Even as a teenager, I had questions about sex. When I had intercourse for the first time, at the age of eighteen, I already knew what orgasm felt like from masturbation. I immediately realised the huge deception of pornography and erotic fiction. Yet even though it was my experience, there was always the doubt that other women might respond differently. Our adult culture, of exaggerating women's erotic response, is so widespread that it is difficult to ignore. Narrative accounts and visual portrayals of women apparently responding erotically obviously arouse men but they also appeal to women's vanity.

Later I appreciated that although my disappointment over sex was personal to me as a woman, it was ironically more of an issue for men. Men want to believe beyond all logic that women want sex as much as they do because sex is so important to them. The trouble with this deception (men's refusal to accept women for what they are) is that it pushes the responsibility back onto women. It's as if men blame women for being the way they are. Men essentially insist that women must be (by pretending or faking) what men want them to be. This makes sex even harder for a woman. She either has to fake or she has to find other ways of making sex exciting for a man.

Years later when I sought advice, I was shocked by the defensive attitudes and misinformation I met with. When I consulted therapists, they claimed to have no idea what I was talking about. I slowly concluded that most women never notice that anything is missing from sex. If you experience something (such as orgasm) that is significant, you are motivated to compare notes with others. But when you find other women are unwilling to discuss the topic, you want to reassure younger women with similar experiences, that they are not alone. This has been my prime motivation for writing about sexuality. I am driven by a desire to correct the sexual ignorance that I have had to face, which has made finding answers much more embarrassing than it needed to be. It should be a basic right for everyone to have access to unbiased sex information.

Realising that the experience is rare, I have been explicit. By providing a detailed account, I hope to differentiate myself from all the fictional stories about women's supposed responsiveness. I have gradually assumed a position of authority because I have never met anyone else who can talk about sexuality in the explicit and objective way that I think is necessary. Overall, I have probably made as much of a mess of things as the next person. I have not been a model for others but I have persevered where someone else might perhaps, quite reasonably, have given up. I have struggled where others would have sensibly accepted defeat and moved on.

I have the intellect to challenge the status quo and the courage to demand answers. I am motivated to put the picture straight. I differentiate between erotic fiction and the much less popular facts and logical reasoning that support a scientific understanding of our sexuality. My conclusions are not gospel. They are deductions I believe to be valid after many years of researching the topic. I have made my conclusions available via the internet in order to reach as many people as possible. No one can benefit from truths they are not ready to hear. The information I provide is for those who appreciate it because they themselves are looking for answers.

I grew up with an interest in science. I wasn't especially good at it but the concepts fascinated me. One of the issues that I understood to be core to scientific knowledge was the concept of a proof. A theory is proposed on the basis of strong evidence or logic. Then scientists challenge the theory until the weight of supporting evidence means that it is accepted as part of scientific knowledge. This does not happen in sexology. Papers are written in language designed to obfuscate the discussion. There is no forum where thinking adults can ask questions or compare notes about sex. No organisation disseminates explanations or research findings. We don't even have a comprehensive account of human sexuality.

The vast majority of people just have sex. This is not really experience of anything much. So-called sex experts are people who are happy to discuss intimacy and personal issues. They talk about sexual health, reproduction and relationships. You cannot give someone the ability to understand sexuality. Our appreciation of sexuality depends on two factors. Firstly, it helps if we have some experience of responsiveness (primarily a male characteristic). Secondly, we need the communication skills, sense of adventure and willingness to explore sex play with a lover over decades.

There is a misconception that to be an authority on sexuality, we must have attended an academic course. But what facts, logic and research findings are these courses based on? Sexologists do not support their academic opinions with research findings any more than anyone else. The general public never questions this lack of factual and logical evidence. Research that challenges the emotional beliefs of the general public obtains very little support and funding.

I'm glad to say that I'm not an expert. I haven't been trained in the sexual ignorance that others are willing to accept. I have relied on my common sense. I have been able to explain my experiences in terms of the research findings. The overwhelming proof of my competency is that I am ready to talk about explicit aspects of sexuality. Very few people worldwide (via the internet) have anything explicit or constructive to say on the topic. No one seems to appreciate that original research has to change the status quo. It does not involve simply agreeing with everyone else's opinions.

I am certainly educated and intelligent enough to acquire the relevant academic qualifications. But I could not sit passively through a course that provides misinformation about women's sexuality. I would never find a research sponsor because I am challenging current beliefs that bolster men's view of their role in providing women with sexual pleasure through intercourse. Very few people are interested in women's sexual experiences that do not conform to women's sexual and social role of pleasing men.

If current beliefs about women's sexuality were largely correct with only a few factual errors, I could join one of these institutions and work with them to correct the misunderstandings. But the errors and misconceptions are so colossal and all-encompassing that no one is going to listen from within. Every institution is dominated by the male viewpoint because men, being so much more interested in sexuality, constitute the prime consumer. The women, who take part, mirror the male view because this is the only way to have a paying job in sexology. My research focuses on asking difficult questions and is much less popular. I am prepared to be judged on the usefulness of my work to the general public and sex educators.

In the beginning I hoped that someone would join me. I thought that sexually experienced women, perhaps lesbians or prostitutes would have something to say. Very few people are motivated by a scientific understanding of sexuality. There's no money in it and everyone has to earn a living. I am motivated by my determination to document the truth. The advantage of being outside professional bodies is that I am independent. I have a unique position of being able to ask unpopular questions and discuss the topic without the threat of censure. This is vital for the work that I have set myself.

www.ingramcontent.com/pod-product-compliance
Lightning Source LLC
Chambersburg PA
CBHW061323040426
42444CB00011B/2745